Casenote Legal Briefs

CRIMINAL PROCEDURE

Adaptable to utilizing Allen, Kuhns and Stuntz' casebook on
Constitutional Criminal Procedure

NORMAN S. GOLDENBERG, SENIOR EDITOR
PETER TENEN, MANAGING EDITOR

STAFF WRITERS
KEMP RICHARDSON
MICHAEL LECONTE
STEPHEN BENARDO
JENNIFER RICK

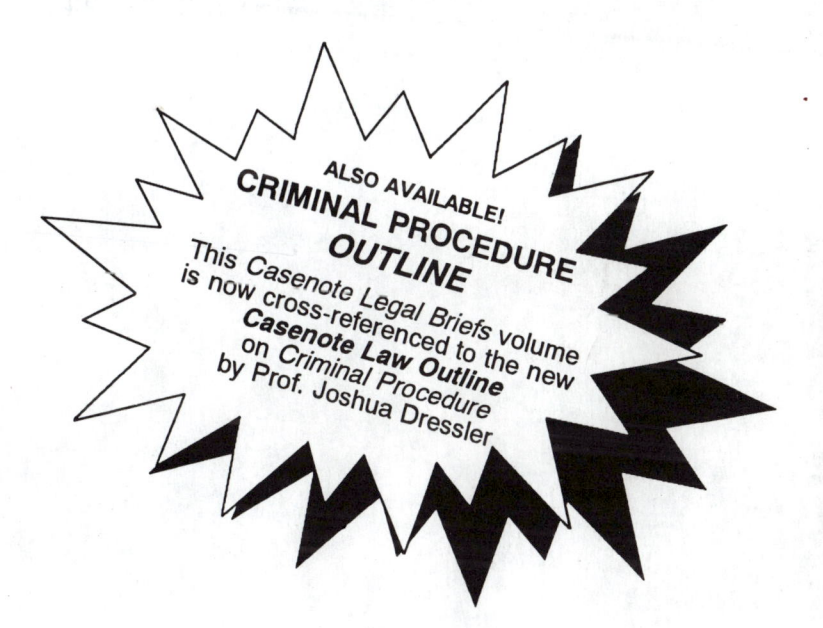

ALSO AVAILABLE!
CRIMINAL PROCEDURE OUTLINE
This Casenote Legal Briefs volume is now cross-referenced to the new *Casenote Law Outline on Criminal Procedure* by Prof. Joshua Dressler

PUBLISHED BY   CASENOTES PUBLISHING CO., INC. 1640 5th ST., SUITE 208   SANTA MONICA, CA 90401

Copyright © 1995 by Casenotes Publishing Co., Inc.
All rights reserved. No part of this book may be reproduced in any form or by any electronic or mechanical means including information storage and retrieval system without permission from the publisher.

ISBN 0-87457-195-2

FORMAT FOR THE CASENOTE LEGAL BRIEF

CASE CAPSULE: This boldface section (first three paragraphs) highlights the procedural nature of the case, a short summary of the facts, and the rule of law. This is an invaluable quick-review device designed to refresh the student's memory for classroom discussion and exam preparation.

NATURE OF CASE: This section identifies the form of action (e.g., breach of contract, negligence, battery), the type of proceeding (e.g., demurrer, appeal from trial court's jury instructions) and the relief sought (e.g., damages, injunction, criminal sanctions).

FACT SUMMARY: The fact summary is included to refresh the student's memory. It can be used as a quick reminder of the facts when the student is chosen by an instructor to brief a case.

CONCISE RULE OF LAW: This portion of the brief summarizes the general principle of law that the case illustrates. Like the fact summary, it is included to refresh the student's memory. It may be used for instant recall of the court's holding and for classroom discussion or home review.

FACTS: This section contains all relevant facts of the case, including the contentions of the parties and the lower court holdings. It is written in a logical order to give the student a clear understanding of the case. The plaintiff and defendant are identified by their proper names throughout and are always labeled with a (P) or (D).

ISSUE: The issue is a concise question that brings out the essence of the opinion as it relates to the section of the casebook in which the case appears. Both substantive and procedural issues are included if relevant to the decision.

HOLDING AND DECISION: This section offers a clear and in-depth discussion of the rule of the case and the court's rationale. It is written in easy-to-understand language. When relevant, it includes a thorough discussion of the exceptions listed by the court, the concurring and dissenting opinions, and the names of the judges.

CONCURRENCE / DISSENT: All concurrences and dissents are briefed whenever they are included by the casebook editor.

EDITOR'S ANALYSIS: This last paragraph gives the student a broad understanding of where the case "fits in" with other cases in the section of the book and with the entire course. It is a hornbook-style discussion indicating whether the case is a majority or minority opinion and comparing the principal case with other cases in the casebook. It may also provide analysis from restatements, uniform codes, and law review articles. The editor's analysis will prove to be invaluable to classroom discussion.

CROSS-REFERENCE TO OUTLINE: Wherever possible, following each case is a cross-reference linking the subject matter of the issue to the appropriate place in the *Casenote Law Outline*, which provides further information on the subject.

WINTER v. G.P. PUTNAM'S SONS
938 F.2d 1033 (1991).

NATURE OF CASE: Appeal from summary judgment in a products liability action.

FACT SUMMARY: Winter (P) relied on a book on mushrooms published by Putnam (D) and became critically ill after eating a poisonous mushroom.

CONCISE RULE OF LAW: Strict products liability is not applicable to the expressions contained within a book.

FACTS: Winter (P) purchased The Encyclopedia of Mushrooms, a book published by Putnam (D), to help in collecting and eating wild mushrooms. In 1988, Winter (P), relying on descriptions in the book, ate some wild mushrooms which turned out to be poisonous. Winter (P) became so ill he required a liver transplant. He brought a strict products liability action against Putnam (D), alleging that the book contained erroneous and misleading information that caused his injury. Putnam (D) responded that the information in the book was not a product for purposes of strict products liability, and the trial court granted its motion for summary judgment. The trial court also rejected Winter's (P) actions for negligence and misrepresentation. Winter (P) appealed.

ISSUE: Is strict products liability applicable to the expressions contained within a book?

HOLDING AND DECISION: (Sneed, J.) No. Strict products liability is not applicable to the expressions contained within a book. Products liability is geared toward tangible objects. The expression of ideas is governed by copyright, libel, and misrepresentation laws. The Restatement (Second) of Torts lists examples of the items that are covered by §402A strict liability. All are tangible items, such as tires or automobiles. There is no indication that the doctrine should be expanded beyond this area. Furthermore, there is a strong public interest in the unfettered exchange of ideas. The threat of liability without fault could seriously inhibit persons who wish to share thoughts and ideas with others. Although some courts have held that aeronautical charts are products for purposes of strict liability, these charts are highly technical tools which resemble compasses. The Encyclopedia of Mushrooms, published by Putnam (D), is a book of pure thought and expression and therefore does not constitute a product for purposes of strict liability. Additionally, publishers do not owe a duty to investigate the contents of books that they distribute. Therefore, a negligence action may not be maintained by Winter (P) against Putnam (D). Affirmed.

EDITOR'S ANALYSIS: This decision is in accord with the rulings in most jurisdictions. See Alm v. Nostrand Reinhold Co., Inc., 480 N.E. 2d 1263 (Ill. 1985). The court also stated that since the publisher is not a guarantor of the accuracy of an author's statements, an action for negligent misrepresentation could not be maintained. The elements of negligent misrepresentation are stated in § 311 of the Restatement (Second) of Torts.

[For more information on misrepresentation, see Casenote Law Outline on Torts, Chapter 12, § III, Negligent Misrepresentation.]

NOTE TO STUDENT

OUR GOAL. It is the goal of Casenotes Publishing Company, Inc. to create and distribute the finest, clearest and most accurate legal briefs available. To this end, we are constantly seeking new ideas, comments and constructive criticism. As a user of *Casenote Legal Briefs,* your suggestions will be highly valued. With all correspondence, please include your complete name, address, and telephone number, including area code and zip code.

THE TOTAL STUDY SYSTEM. Casenote Legal Briefs are just one part of the Casenotes TOTAL STUDY SYSTEM. Most briefs are (wherever possible) cross-referenced to the appropriate *Casenote Law Outline,* which will elaborate on the issue at hand. By purchasing a Law Outline together with your Legal Brief, you will have both parts of the Casenotes TOTAL STUDY SYSTEM. (See the advertising in the front of this book for a list of Law Outlines currently available.)

A NOTE ABOUT LANGUAGE. Please note that the language used in *Casenote Legal Briefs* in reference to minority groups and women reflects terminology used within the historical context of the time in which the respective courts wrote the opinions. We at Casenotes Publishing Co., Inc. are well aware of and very sensitive to the desires of all people to be treated with dignity and to be referred to as they prefer. Because such preferences change from time to time, and because the language of the courts reflects the time period in which opinions were written, our case briefs will not necessarily reflect contemporary references. We appreciate your understanding and invite your comments.

A NOTE REGARDING NEW EDITIONS. As of our press date, this Casenote Legal Brief is current and includes briefs of all cases in the current version of the casebook, divided into chapters that correspond to that edition of the casebook. However, occasionally a new edition of the casebook comes out in the interim, and sometimes the casebook author will make changes in the sequence of the cases in the chapters, add or delete cases, or change the chapter titles. Should you be using this Legal Brief in conjuction with a casebook that was issued later than this book, you can receive all of the newer cases, which are available free from us, by sending in the "Supplement Request Form" in this section of the book (please follow all instructions on that form). The Supplement(s) will contain all the missing cases, and will bring your Casenote Legal Brief up to date.

EDITOR'S NOTE. Casenote Legal Briefs are intended to supplement the student's casebook, not replace it. There is no substitute for the student's own mastery of this important learning and study technique. If used properly, *Casenote Legal Briefs* are an effective law study aid that will serve to reinforce the student's understanding of the cases.

REF. #1205-95-898

SUPPLEMENT REQUEST FORM

At the time this book was printed, a brief was included for every major case in the casebook and for everyy existing supplement to the casebook. However, if a new supplement to the casebook (or a new edition of the casebook) has been published since this publication was printed and if that casebook supplement (or new edition of the casebook) was available for sale at the time you purchased this Casenote Legal Briefs book, we will be pleased to provide you the new cases contained therein AT NO CHARGE when you send us a stamped, self-addressed envelope.

TO OBTAIN YOUR FREE SUPPLEMENT MATERIAL, **YOU MUST FOLLOW THE INSTRUCTIONS BELOW PRECISELY** OR YOUR REQUEST WILL NOT BE ACKNOWLEDGED!

1. Please check if there is in fact an existing supplement and, if so, that the cases are not already included in your Casenote Legal Briefs. Check the main table of cases as well as the supplement table of cases, if any.

2. **REMOVE THIS ENTIRE PAGE FROM THE BOOK.** You MUST send this ORIGINAL page to receive your supplement. This page acts as your proof of purchase and contains the reference number necessary to fill your supplement request properly. No photocopy of this page or written request will be honored or answered. Any request from which the reference number has been removed, altered or obliterated will not be honored.

★ 3. Prepare a STAMPED self-addressed envelope for return mailing. Be sure to use a FULL SIZE (9 X 12) ENVELOPE (MANILA TYPE) so that the supplement will fit and AFFIX ENOUGH POSTAGE TO COVER 3 OZ. **ANY SUPPLEMENT REQUEST NOT ACCOMPANIED BY A STAMPED SELF-ADDRESSED ENVELOPE WILL ABSOLUTELY NOT BE FILLED OR ACKNOWLEDGED.**

4. MULTIPLE SUPPLEMENT REQUESTS: If you are ordering more than one supplement, we suggest that you enclose a stamped, self-addressed envelope for each supplement requested. If you enclose only one envelope for a multiple request, your order may not be filled immediately should any supplement which you requested still be in production. In other words, your order will be held by us until it can be filled completely.

5. Casenotes prints two kinds of supplements. A "New Edition" supplement is issued when a new edition of your casebook is published. A "New Edition" supplement gives you all major cases found in the new edition of the casebook which did not appear in the previous edition. A regular "supplement" is issued when a paperback supplement to your casebook is published. If the box at the lower right is stamped, then the "New Edition" supplement was provided to your bookstore and is *not* available from Casenotes; however, Casenotes will still send you any regular "supplements" which have been printed either before or after the new edition of your casebook appeared and which, according to the reference number at the top of this page, have not been included in this book. If the box is not stamped, Casenotes will send you any supplements, "New Edition" and/or regular, needed to completely update your Casenote Legal Briefs.

★ ☞ NOTE: REQUESTS FOR SUPPLEMENTS WILL NOT BE FILLED UNLESS THESE INSTRUCTIONS ARE COMPLIED WITH!

6. Fill in the following information:

Full title of CASEBOOK ___ **CRIMINAL PROCEDURE**

CASEBOOK author's name ___ **Allen, Kuhns and Stuntz**

Copyright year of new edition or new paperback supplement

Name and location of bookstore where this Casenote Legal Brief was purchased ___

Name and location of law school you attend ___

Any comments regarding Casenote Legal Briefs ___

NOTE: IF THIS BOX IS STAMPED, NO NEW EDITION SUPPLEMENT CAN BE OBTAINED BY MAIL.

PUBLISHED BY CASENOTES PUBLISHING CO., INC. 1640 5th ST, SUITE 208 SANTA MONICA, CA 90401

PLEASE PRINT
NAME ___ **PHONE** ___ **DATE** ___
ADDRESS/CITY/STATE/ZIP ___

Announcing the First *Totally Integrated* Law Study System

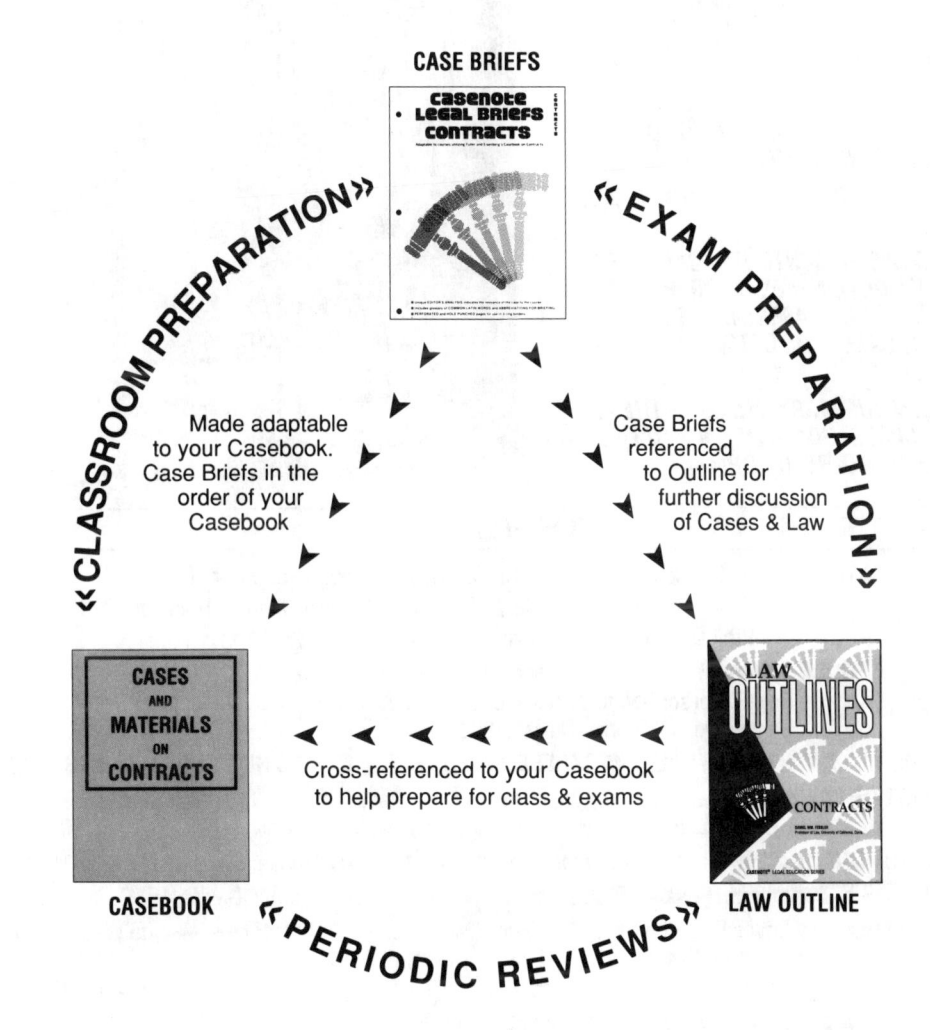

CASE BRIEFS

«CLASSROOM PREPARATION»

Made adaptable to your Casebook. Case Briefs in the order of your Casebook

«EXAM PREPARATION»

Case Briefs referenced to Outline for further discussion of Cases & Law

CASEBOOK

Cross-referenced to your Casebook to help prepare for class & exams

LAW OUTLINE

«PERIODIC REVIEWS»

Casenotes Integrated Study System Makes Studying Easier and More Effective Than Ever!

Casenotes has just made studying easier and more effective than ever before, because we've done the work for you! Through our exclusive integrated study system, most briefs found in this volume of Casenote Legal Briefs are cross-referenced to the corresponding area of law in the Casenote Law Outline series. The cross-reference immediately follows the Editor's Analysis at the end of the brief, and it will direct you to the corresponding chapter and section number in the Casenote Law Outline for further information on the case or the area of law.

This cross-referencing feature will enable you to make the most effective use of your time. While each Casenote Law Outline focuses on a particular subject area of the law, each legal briefs volume is adapted to a specific casebook. Now, with cross-referencing of Casenote Legal Briefs to Casenote Law Outlines, you can have the best of both worlds – briefs for all major cases in your casebooks and easy-to-find, easy-to-read explanations of the law in our Law Outline series. Casenote Law Outlines are authored exclusively by law professors who are nationally recognized authorities in their field. So using Casenote Law Outlines is like studying with the top law professors.

Try Casenotes new totally integrated study system and see just how easy and effective studying can be.

Casenotes Integrated Study System Does The Work For You!

LAW OUTLINES from CASENOTE™
the Ultimate Outline

▶ **WRITTEN BY NATIONALLY RECOGNIZED AUTHORITIES IN THEIR FIELD.**

▶ **FEATURING A FLEXIBLE, SUBJECT-ORIENTED APPROACH.**

▶ **CONTAINS: TABLE OF CONTENTS; CAPSULE OUTLINE; FULL OUTLINE; EXAM PREPARATION; GLOSSARY; TABLE OF CASES; TABLE OF AUTHORITIES; CASEBOOK CROSS REFERENCE CHART; INDEX.**

▶ **THE TOTAL LAW SUMMARY UTILIZING THE MOST COMPREHENSIVE STUDY APPROACH IN THE MOST EFFECTIVE, EASY-TO-READ FORMAT.**

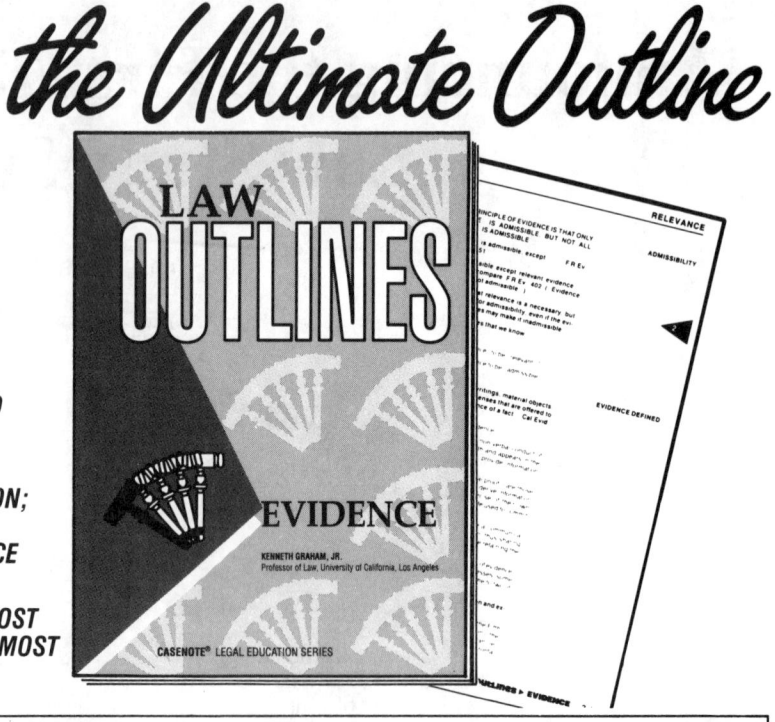

REF #	SUBJECT / AUTHORS	RETAIL PRICE
#5260	**ADMINISTRATIVE LAW** by **Charles H. Koch, Jr.,** Dudley W. Woodbridge Professor of Law, College of William and Mary. **Sidney A. Shapiro,** John M. Rounds Professor of Law, University of Kansas. (1996 w/'98 supp.)	(effective 7/1/98) $20.95
#5040	**CIVIL PROCEDURE** by **John B. Oakley,** Professor of Law, University of California, Davis. **Rex R. Perschbacher,** Professor of Law & Associate Dean, Academic Affairs, University of California, Davis. (1996)	$21.95
	COMMERCIAL LAW (see 5700 SALES ● 5710 SECURED TRANS. ● 5720 NEG. INSTRUMENTS & PMT. SYST.)	
#5070	**CONFLICT OF LAWS** by **Luther L. McDougal, III,** W.R. Irby Professor of Law, Tulane University. **Robert L. Felix,** James P. Mozingo, III, Prof. of Law, Univ. of S. Carolina. (1996)	$20.95
#5080	**CONSTITUTIONAL LAW** by **Gary Goodpaster,** Prof. of Law, Univ. of California, Davis. (1997 w/'98 supp.)	$23.95
#5010	**CONTRACTS** by **Daniel Wm. Fessler,** Professor of Law, University of California, Davis. (1996)	$20.95
#5050	**CORPORATIONS AND ALTERNATIVE BUSINESS VEHICLES** by **Lewis D. Solomon,** Arthur Selwin Miller Research Prof. of Law, George Washington Univ. **Daniel Wm. Fessler,** Prof. of Law, University of California, Davis. **Arthur E. Wilmarth, Jr.,** Assoc. Prof. of Law, George Washington University. (1997)	$23.95
#5020	**CRIMINAL LAW** by **Joshua Dressler,** Professor of Law, McGeorge School of Law. (1996)	$20.95
#5200	**CRIMINAL PROCEDURE** by **Joshua Dressler,** Prof. of Law, McGeorge School of Law. (1997)	$19.95
#5800	**ESTATE & GIFT TAX** INCLUDING THE FEDERAL GENERATION-SKIPPING TAX by **Joseph M. Dodge,** W.H. Francis Prof. of Law, University of Texas at Austin (w/ supp. due Fall 1998)	$20.95
#5060	**EVIDENCE** by **Kenneth Graham, Jr.,** Professor of Law, University of California, Los Angeles. (1996)	$22.95
#5400	**FEDERAL COURTS** by **Howard P. Fink,** Isadore and Ida Topper Prof. of Law, Ohio State University. **Linda S. Mullenix,** Bernard J. Ward Centennial Prof. of Law, Univ. of Texas. (1997)	$21.95
#5210	**FEDERAL INCOME TAXATION** by **Joseph M. Dodge,** W.H. Francis Professor of Law, University of Texas at Austin (1998).	$21.95
#5300	**LEGAL RESEARCH** by **Nancy L. Schultz,** Associate Professor of Law, Chapman University. **Louis J. Sirico, Jr.,** Professor of Law, Villanova University. (1996)	$20.95
#5720	**NEGOTIABLE INST. & PMT. SYST.** by **Donald B. King,** Professor of Law, Saint Louis University. **Peter Winship,** James Cleo Thompson, Sr. Trustee Prof., SMU. (1995)	$21.95
#5030	**PROPERTY** by **Sheldon F. Kurtz,** Percy Bordwell Professor of Law, University of Iowa. **Patricia Cain,** Professor of Law, University of Iowa (1997)	$21.95
#5700	**SALES** by **Robert E. Scott,** Dean and Lewis F. Powell, Jr. Professor of Law, University of Virginia. **Donald B. King,** Professor of Law, Saint Louis University. (1992)	$20.95
#5710	**SECURED TRANSACTIONS** by **Donald B. King,** Professor of Law, Saint Louis University. (1995 w/'96 supp.)	$19.95
#5000	**TORTS** by **George C. Christie,** James B. Duke Professor of Law, Duke University. **Jerry J. Phillips,** W.P. Toms Professor of Law & Chair, Committee on Admissions, University of Tennessee. (1996 w/'98 supp.)	$21.95
#5220	**WILLS, TRUSTS & ESTATES** by **William M. McGovern,** Professor of Law, University of California, Los Angeles. (1996)	$21.95

rev. 6/1/98

CASENOTE LEGAL BRIEFS

PRICE LIST EFFECTIVE JULY 1, 1998 • PRICES SUBJECT TO CHANGE WITHOUT NOTICE

Ref. No.	Course	Adaptable to Courses Utilizing	Retail Price
1263	ADMINISTRATIVE LAW	BREYER, STEWART & SUNSTEIN	20.00
1266	ADMINISTRATIVE LAW	CASS, DIVER & BEERMAN	18.00
1260	ADMINISTRATIVE LAW	GELLHORN, B., S., R., S. & F.	18.00
1264	ADMINISTRATIVE LAW	MASHAW, MERRILL & SHANE	19.50
1267	ADMINISTRATIVE LAW	REESE	18.00
1262	ADMINISTRATIVE LAW	SCHWARTZ	19.00
1350	AGENCY & PARTNERSHIP (ENT.ORG)	CONARD, KNAUSS & SIEGEL	22.00
1351	AGENCY & PARTNERSHIP	HYNES	21.00
1690	AMERICAN INDIAN LAW	GETCHES, W. & W.	TBA
1281	ANTITRUST (TRADE REGULATION)	HANDLER, P., G. & W.	18.50
1280	ANTITRUST	AREEDA & KAPLOW	17.50
1283	ANTITRUST	SULLIVAN & HOVENKAMP	19.00
1611	BANKING LAW	MACEY & MILLER	18.00
1303	BANKRUPTCY (DEBTOR-CREDITOR)	EISENBERG	20.00
1305	BANKRUPTCY	JORDAN & WARREN	18.00
1058	BUSINESS ASSOCIATIONS (CORPORATIONS)	KLEIN & RAMSEYER	20.00
1040	CIVIL PROCEDURE	COUND, F., M. & S	21.00
1043	CIVIL PROCEDURE	FIELD, KAPLAN & CLERMONT	21.00
1049	CIVIL PROCEDURE	FREER & PERDUE	17.00
1041	CIVIL PROCEDURE	HAZARD, TAIT & FLETCHER	20.00
1047	CIVIL PROCEDURE	MARCUS, REDISH & SHERMAN	20.00
1044	CIVIL PROCEDURE	ROSENBERG, S. & D.	21.00
1046	CIVIL PROCEDURE	YEAZELL	18.00
1311	COMM'L LAW	FARNSWORTH, H., R, H. & M.	20.00
1312	COMM'L LAW	JORDAN & WARREN	20.00
1310	COMM'L LAW (SALES/SEC.TR./PAY.LAW [Sys.])	SPEIDEL, SUMMERS & WHITE	23.00
1313	COMM'L LAW (SALES/SEC.TR./PAY.LAW)	WHALEY	21.00
1320	COMMUNITY PROPERTY	BIRD	18.50
1630	COMPARATIVE LAW	SCHLESINGER, B., D., H.& W.	17.00
1048	COMPLEX LITIGATION	MARCUS & SHERMAN	18.00
1072	CONFLICTS	BRILMAYER	18.00
1071	CONFLICTS	CRAMTON, C. K., & K.	18.00
1070	CONFLICTS	ROSENBERG, HAY & W.	21.00
1086	CONSTITUTIONAL LAW	BREST & LEVINSON	19.00
1082	CONSTITUTIONAL LAW	COHEN & VARAT	22.00
1088	CONSTITUTIONAL LAW	FARBER, ESKRIDGE & FRICKEY	19.00
1080	CONSTITUTIONAL LAW	GUNTHER & SULLIVAN	21.00
1081	CONSTITUTIONAL LAW	LOCKHART, K., C., S. & F.	19.00
1085	CONSTITUTIONAL LAW	ROTUNDA	21.00
1089	CONSTITUTIONAL LAW (FIRST AMENDMENT)	SHIFFRIN & CHOPER	16.00
1087	CONSTITUTIONAL LAW	STONE, S., S. & T.	20.00
1103	CONTRACTS	BARNETT	22.00
1102	CONTRACTS	BURTON	21.00
1017	CONTRACTS	CALAMARI, PERILLO & BENDER	24.00
1101	CONTRACTS	CRANDALL & WHALEY	21.00
1014	CONTRACTS	DAWSON, HARVEY & H.	20.00
1010	CONTRACTS	FARNSWORTH & YOUNG	19.00
1011	CONTRACTS	FULLER & EISENBERG	22.00
1100	CONTRACTS	HAMILTON, RAU & WEINTRAUB	20.00
1013	CONTRACTS	KESSLER, GILMORE & KRONMAN	24.00
1016	CONTRACTS	KNAPP & CRYSTAL	21.50
1012	CONTRACTS	MURPHY & SPEIDEL	23.00
1018	CONTRACTS	MURRAY	23.00
1015	CONTRACTS	ROSETT	22.00
1019	CONTRACTS	VERNON	21.00
1502	COPYRIGHT	GOLDSTEIN	19.00
1501	COPYRIGHT	NIMMER, M., M. & N.	20.50
1218	CORPORATE TAXATION	LIND, S. L. & R	15.00
1050	CORPORATIONS	CARY & EISENBERG	20.00
1054	CORPORATIONS	CHOPER, COFFEE, & GILSON	22.50
1350	CORPORATIONS (ENTERPRISE ORG.)	CONARD, KNAUSS & SIEGEL	22.00
1053	CORPORATIONS	HAMILTON	20.00
1058	CORPORATIONS (BUSINESS ASSOCIATIONS)	KLEIN & RAMSEYER	20.00
1057	CORPORATIONS	O'KELLEY & THOMPSON	19.00
1056	CORPORATIONS	SOLOMON, S., B. & W.	20.00
1052	CORPORATIONS	VAGTS	19.00
1300	CREDITOR'S RIGHTS (DEBTOR-CREDITOR)	RIESENFELD	22.00
1550	CRIMINAL JUSTICE	WEINREB	19.00
1029	CRIMINAL LAW	BONNIE, C., J. & L.	18.00
1020	CRIMINAL LAW	BOYCE & PERKINS	23.00
1028	CRIMINAL LAW	DRESSLER	22.00
1027	CRIMINAL LAW	JOHNSON	21.00
1021	CRIMINAL LAW	KADISH & SCHULHOFER	20.00
1026	CRIMINAL LAW	KAPLAN, WEISBERG & BINDER	19.00
1205	CRIMINAL PROCEDURE	ALLEN, KUHNS & STUNTZ	18.00
1202	CRIMINAL PROCEDURE	HADDAD, Z., S. & B.	21.00
1200	CRIMINAL PROCEDURE	KAMISAR, LAFAVE & ISRAEL	20.00
1204	CRIMINAL PROCEDURE	SALTZBURG & CAPRA	18.00
1203	CRIMINAL PROCEDURE (PROCESS)	WEINREB	19.50
1303	DEBTOR-CREDITOR	EISENBERG	20.00
1300	DEBTOR-CREDITOR (CRED. RTS.)	RIESENFELD	22.00
1304	DEBTOR-CREDITOR	WARREN & WESTBROOK	20.00
1224	DECEDENTS ESTATES (TRUSTS)	RITCHIE, A, & E.(DOBRIS & STERK).	22.00
1222	DECEDENTS ESTATES	SCOLES & HALBACH	22.50
1231	DECEDENTS ESTATES (TRUSTS)	WAGGONER, A. & F.	21.00
	DOMESTIC RELATIONS (see FAMILY LAW)		
3000	EDUCATION LAW (COURSE OUTLINE)	AQUILA & PETZKE	26.50
1670	EMPLOYMENT DISCRIMINATION	FRIEDMAN & STRICKLER	18.00
1671	EMPLOYMENT DISCRIMINATION	ZIMMER, SULLIVAN, R. & C.	19.00
1660	EMPLOYMENT LAW	ROTHSTEIN, KNAPP & LIEBMAN	20.50
1350	ENTERPRISE ORGANIZATION	CONARD, KNAUSS & SIEGEL	22.00
1342	ENVIRONMENTAL LAW	ANDERSON, MANDELKER & T.	17.00
1341	ENVIRONMENTAL LAW	FINDLEY & FARBER	19.00
1345	ENVIRONMENTAL LAW	MENELL & STEWART	18.00
1344	ENVIRONMENTAL LAW	PERCIVAL, MILLER, S. & L.	19.00
1343	ENVIRONMENTAL LAW	PLATER, A., G. & G.	18.00
	EQUITY (see REMEDIES)		
1217	ESTATE & GIFT TAXATION	BITTKER, CLARK & McCOUCH	16.00
	ETHICS (see PROFESSIONAL RESPONSIBILITY)		
1065	EVIDENCE	GREEN & NESSON	21.00
1066	EVIDENCE	MUELLER & KIRKPATRICK	18.00
1064	EVIDENCE	STRONG, BROUN & M.	23.50
1062	EVIDENCE	SUTTON & WELLBORN	23.00
1061	EVIDENCE	WALTZ & PARK	21.00
1060	EVIDENCE	WEINSTEIN, M., A. & B.	23.50
1244	FAMILY LAW (DOMESTIC RELATIONS)	AREEN	23.00
1242	FAMILY LAW (DOMESTIC RELATIONS)	CLARK & GLOWINSKY	20.00
1245	FAMILY LAW (DOMESTIC RELATIONS)	ELLMAN, KURTZ & BARTLETT	21.00
1246	FAMILY LAW (DOMESTIC RELATIONS)	HARRIS, T. & W.	20.00
1243	FAMILY LAW (DOMESTIC RELATIONS)	KRAUSE, O., E. & G.	25.00
1240	FAMILY LAW (DOMESTIC RELATIONS)	WADLINGTON	21.00
1231	FAMILY PROPERTY LAW (WILLS/TRUSTS)	WAGGONER, A. & F.	21.00
1360	FEDERAL COURTS	FALLON, M. & S. (HART & W.)	20.00
1360	FEDERAL COURTS	HART & WECHSLER (FALLON)	20.00
1363	FEDERAL COURTS	LOW & JEFFRIES	17.00
1361	FEDERAL COURTS	McCORMICK, C. & W.	21.00
1364	FEDERAL COURTS	REDISH & SHERRY	18.00
1089	FIRST AMENDMENT (CONSTITUTIONAL LAW)	SHIFFRIN & CHOPER	16.00
1510	GRATUITOUS TRANSFERS	CLARK, LUSKY & MURPHY	19.00
1650	HEALTH LAW	FURROW, J., J. & S.	18.50
1640	IMMIGRATION LAW	ALEINIKOFF, MARTIN & M.	17.00
1641	IMMIGRATION LAW	LEGOMSKY	20.00
1690	INDIAN LAW (AMERICAN)	GETCHES, W. & W.	TBA
1371	INSURANCE LAW	KEETON	22.00
1372	INSURANCE LAW	YORK, WHELAN & MARTINEZ	20.00
1370	INSURANCE LAW	YOUNG & HOLMES	18.00
1394	INTERNATIONAL BUSINESS TRANSACTIONS	FOLSOM, GORDON & SPANOGLE	16.00
1393	INTERNATIONAL LAW	CARTER & TRIMBLE	17.00
1392	INTERNATIONAL LAW	HENKIN, P., S. & S.	18.00
1390	INTERNATIONAL LAW	OLIVER, F., B., S. & W.	23.00
1331	LABOR LAW	COX, BOK, GORMAN & FINKIN	20.00
1332	LABOR LAW	HARPER & ESTREICHER	21.00
1333	LABOR LAW	LESLIE	19.50
1330	LABOR LAW	MERRIFIELD, S. & C.	20.00
1471	LAND FINANCE (REAL ESTATE TRANS)	BERGER & JOHNSTONE	19.00
1620	LAND FINANCE (REAL ESTATE TRANS)	NELSON & WHITMAN	20.00
1452	LAND USE	CALLIES, FREILICH & ROBERTS	18.00
1421	LEGISLATION	ESKRIDGE & FRICKEY	16.00
1480	MASS MEDIA	FRANKLIN & ANDERSON	16.00
1312	NEGOTIABLE INSTRUMENTS (COMM. LAW)	JORDAN & WARREN	20.00
1541	OIL & GAS	KUNTZ, L. A. & S.	19.00
1540	OIL & GAS	MAXWELL, WILLIAMS, M. & K.	19.00
1560	PATENT LAW	FRANCIS & COLLINS	24.00
1310	PAYMENT LAW [SYST.][COMM. LAW]	SPEIDEL, SUMMERS & WHITE	23.00
1313	PAYMENT LAW (COMM.LAW / NEG. INST.)	WHALEY	23.00
1431	PRODUCTS LIABILITY	OWEN, MONTGOMERY & K.	23.00
1091	PROF. RESPONSIBILITY (ETHICS)	GILLERS	14.00
1093	PROF. RESPONSIBILITY (ETHICS)	HAZARD, KONIAK, & CRAMTON	19.00
1092	PROF. RESPONSIBILITY (ETHICS)	MORGAN & ROTUNDA	14.00
1030	PROPERTY	CASNER & LEACH	22.00
1031	PROPERTY	CRIBBET, J., F. & S.	22.50
1037	PROPERTY	DONAHUE, KAUPER & MARTIN	19.00
1035	PROPERTY	DUKEMINIER & KRIER	19.00
1034	PROPERTY	HAAR & LIEBMAN	21.50
1036	PROPERTY	KURTZ & HOVENKAMP	20.00
1033	PROPERTY	NELSON, STOEBUCK, & W.	21.50
1032	PROPERTY	RABIN & KWALL	21.00
1038	PROPERTY	SINGER	19.50
1621	REAL ESTATE TRANSACTIONS	GOLDSTEIN & KORNGOLD	19.00
1471	REAL ESTATE TRANS. & FIN. (LAND FINANCE)	BERGER & JOHNSTONE	19.00
1620	REAL ESTATE TRANSFER & FINANCE	NELSON & WHITMAN	19.00
1254	REMEDIES (EQUITY)	LAYCOCK	21.00
1253	REMEDIES (EQUITY)	LEAVELL, L, N. & K/F.	22.00
1252	REMEDIES (EQUITY)	RE & RE	24.00
1255	REMEDIES (EQUITY)	SHOBEN & TABB	23.50
1250	REMEDIES (EQUITY)	YORK, BAUMAN & RENDLEMAN	26.00
1310	SALES (COMM. LAW)	SPEIDEL, SUMMERS & WHITE	23.00
1313	SALES (COMM. LAW)	WHALEY	21.00
1312	SECURED TRANS. (COMM. LAW)	JORDAN & WARREN	20.00
1310	SECURED TRANS.	SPEIDEL, SUMMERS & WHITE	23.00
1313	SECURED TRANS. (COMM. LAW)	WHALEY	21.00
1272	SECURITIES REGULATION	COX, HILLMAN, LANGEVOORT	19.00
1270	SECURITIES REGULATION	JENNINGS, M., C. & S.	19.00
1680	SPORTS LAW	WEILER & ROBERTS	18.50
1217	TAXATION (ESTATE & GIFT)	BITTKER, CLARK & McCOUCH	16.00
1219	TAXATION (INDIV. INC.)	BURKE & FRIEL	20.00
1212	TAXATION (FED. INC.)	FREELAND, LIND & STEPHENS	19.00
1211	TAXATION (FED. INC.)	GRAETZ & SCHENK	18.00
1210	TAXATION (FED. INC.)	KLEIN & BANKMAN	19.00
1218	TAXATION (CORPORATE)	LIND, S., L. & R.	15.00
1006	TORTS	DOBBS	20.00
1003	TORTS	EPSTEIN	21.50
1004	TORTS	FRANKLIN & RABIN	18.50
1001	TORTS	HENDERSON, P. & S.	21.50
1000	TORTS	PROSSER, W., S., & P.	25.00
1005	TORTS	SHULMAN, JAMES & GRAY	23.00
1281	TRADE REGULATION (ANTITRUST)	HANDLER, P., G. & W.	18.50
1230	TRUSTS	BOGERT, O., H. & H.	21.50
1231	TRUSTS/WILLS (FAMILY PROPERTY LAW)	WAGGONER, A. & F.	21.00
1410	U.C.C.	EPSTEIN, MARTIN, H. & N.	16.00
1223	WILLS, TRUSTS & ESTATES	DUKEMINIER & JOHANSON	20.00
1220	WILLS	MECHEM & ATKINSON	21.00
1231	WILLS/TRUSTS (FAMILY PROPERTY LAW)	WAGGONER, A. & F.	21.00

(SERIES XLI)

CASENOTES PUBLISHING CO. INC. ● 1640 FIFTH STREET, SUITE 208 ● SANTA MONICA, CA 90401 ● (310) 395-6500

E-Mail Address- casenote@westworld.com
Website-http://www.casenotes.com

PLEASE PURCHASE FROM YOUR LOCAL BOOKSTORE. IF UNAVAILABLE, YOU MAY ORDER DIRECT.*
4TH CLASS POSTAGE (ALLOW TWO WEEKS) $1.00 PER ORDER; 1ST CLASS POSTAGE $3.00 (ONE BOOK), $2.00 EACH (TWO OR MORE BOOKS)
*CALIF. RESIDENTS PLEASE ADD 8¼% SALES TAX

Notes

HOW TO BRIEF A CASE

A. DECIDE ON A FORMAT AND STICK TO IT

Structure is essential to a good brief. It enables you to arrange systematically the related parts that are scattered throughout most cases, thus making manageable and understandable what might otherwise seem to be an endless and unfathomable sea of information. There are, of course, an unlimited number of formats that can be utilized. However, it is best to find one that suits your needs and stick to it. Consistency breeds both efficiency and the security that when called upon you will know where to look in your brief for the information you are asked to give.

Any format, as long as it presents the essential elements of a case in an organized fashion, can be used. Experience, however, has led *Casenotes* to develop and utilize the following format because of its logical flow and universal applicability.

NATURE OF CASE: This is a brief statement of the legal character and procedural status of the case (e.g., "Appeal of a burglary conviction").

There are many different alternatives open to a litigant dissatisfied with a court ruling. The key to determining which one has been used is to discover *who is asking this court for what*.

This first entry in the brief should be kept as *short as possible*. The student should use the court's terminology if the student understands it. But since jurisdictions vary as to the titles of pleadings, the best entry is the one that apprises the student of who wants what in this proceeding, not the one that sounds most like the court's language.

CONCISE RULE OF LAW: A statement of the general principle of law that the case illustrates (e.g., "An acceptance that varies any term of the offer is considered a rejection and counteroffer").

Determining the rule of law of a case is a procedure similar to determining the issue of the case. Avoid being fooled by red herrings; there may be a few rules of law mentioned in the case excerpt, but usually only one is *the* rule with which the casebook editor is concerned. The techniques used to locate the issue, described below, may also be utilized to find the rule of law. Generally, your best guide is simply the chapter heading. It is a clue to the point the casebook editor seeks to make and should be kept in mind when reading every case in the respective section.

FACTS: A synopsis of only the essential facts of the case, i.e., those bearing upon or leading up to the issue.

The facts entry should be a short statement of the events and transactions that led one party to initiate legal proceedings against another in the first place. While some cases conveniently state the salient facts at the beginning of the decision, in other instances they will have to be culled from hiding places throughout the text, even from concurring and dissenting opinions. Some of the "facts" will often be in dispute and should be so noted. Conflicting evidence may be briefly pointed up. "Hard" facts must be included. Both must be *relevant* in order to be listed in the facts entry. It is impossible to tell what is relevant until the entire case is read, as the ultimate determination of the rights and liabilities of the parties may turn on something buried deep in the opinion.

The facts entry should never be longer than one to three *short* sentences.

It is often helpful to identify the role played by a party in a given context. For example, in a construction contract case the identification of a party as the "contractor" or "builder" alleviates the need to tell that that party was the one who was supposed to have built the house.

It is always helpful, and a good general practice, to identify the "plaintiff" and the "defendant." This may seem elementary and uncomplicated, but, especially in view of the creative editing practiced by some casebook editors, it is sometimes a difficult or even impossible task. Bear in mind that the *party presently* seeking something from this court may not be the plaintiff, and that sometimes only the cross-claim of a defendant is treated in the excerpt. Confusing or misaligning the parties can ruin your analysis and understanding of the case.

ISSUE: A statement of the general legal question answered by or illustrated in the case. For clarity, the issue is best put in the form of a question capable of a "yes" or "no" answer. In reality, the issue is simply the Concise Rule of Law put in the form of a question (e.g., "May an offer be accepted by performance?").

The major problem presented in discerning what is *the* issue in the case is that an opinion usually purports to raise and answer several questions. However, except for rare cases, only one such question is really the issue in the case. Collateral issues not necessary to the resolution of the matter in controversy are handled by the court by language known as *"obiter dictum"* or merely *"dictum."* While dicta may be included later in the brief, it has no place under the issue heading.

To find the issue, the student again asks *who wants what* and then goes on to ask *why did that party succeed or fail in getting it.* Once this is determined, the "why" should be turned into a question.

The complexity of the issues in the cases will vary, but in all cases a single-sentence question should sum up the issue. *In a few cases,* there will be two, or even more rarely, three issues of equal importance to the resolution of the case. Each should be expressed in a single-sentence question.

Since many issues are resolved by a court in coming to a final disposition of a case, the casebook editor will reproduce the portion of the opinion containing the issue or issues most relevant to the area of law under scrutiny. A noted law professor gave this advice: "Close the book; look at the title on the cover." Chances are, if it is Property, the student need not concern himself with whether, for example, the federal government's treatment of the plaintiff's land really raises a federal question sufficient to support jurisdiction on this ground in federal court.

The same rule applies to chapter headings designating sub-areas within the subjects. They tip the student off as to what the text is designed to teach. The cases are arranged in a casebook to show a progression or development of the law, so that the preceding cases may also help.

It is also most important to remember to *read the notes and questions* at the end of a case to determine what the editors wanted the student to have gleaned from it.

HOLDING AND DECISION: This section should succinctly explain the rationale of the court in arriving at its decision. In capsulizing the "reasoning" of the court, it should always include an application of the general rule or rules of law to the specific facts of the case. Hidden justifications come to light in this entry; the reasons for the state of the law, the public policies, the biases and prejudices, those considerations that influence the justices' thinking and, ultimately, the outcome of the case. At the end, there should be a short indication of the disposition or procedural resolution of the case (e.g., "Decision of the trial court for Mr. Smith (P) reversed").

The foregoing format is designed to help you "digest" the reams of case material with which you will be faced in your law school career. Once mastered by practice, it will place at your fingertips the information the authors of your casebooks have sought to impart to you in case-by-case illustration and analysis.

B. BE AS ECONOMICAL AS POSSIBLE IN BRIEFING CASES

Once armed with a format that encourages succinctness, it is as important to be economical with regard to the time spent on the actual reading of the case as it is to be economical in the writing of the brief itself. This does not mean "skimming" a case. Rather, it means reading the case with an "eye" trained to recognize into which "section" of your brief a particular passage or line fits and having a system for quickly and precisely marking the case so that the passages fitting any one particular part of the brief can be easily identified and brought together in a concise and accurate manner when the brief is actually written.

It is of no use to simply repeat everything in the opinion of the court; the student should only record enough information to trigger his or her recollection of what the court said. Nevertheless, an accurate statement of the "law of the case," i.e., the legal principle applied to the facts, is absolutely essential to class preparation and to learning the law under the case method.

To that end, it is important to develop a "shorthand" that you can use to make margin notations. These notations will tell you at a glance in which section of the brief you will be placing that particular passage or portion of the opinion.

Some students prefer to underline all the salient portions of the opinion (with a pencil or colored underliner marker), making marginal notations as they go along. Others prefer the color-coded method of underlining, utilizing different colors of markers to underline the salient portions of the case, each separate color being used to represent a different section of the brief. For example, blue underlining could be used for passages relating to the concise rule of law, yellow for those relating to the issue, and green for those relating to the holding and decision, etc. While it has its advocates, the color-coded method can be confusing and time-consuming (all that time spent on changing colored markers). Furthermore, it can interfere with the continuity and concentration many students deem essential to the reading of a case for maximum comprehension. In the end, however, it is a matter of personal preference and style. Just remember, whatever method you use, underlining must be used sparingly or its value is lost.

For those who take the marginal notation route, an efficient and easy method is to go along underlining the key portions of the case and placing in the margin alongside them the following "markers" to indicate where a particular passage or line "belongs" in the brief you will write:

- N (NATURE OF CASE)
- CR (CONCISE RULE OF LAW)
- I (ISSUE)
- HC (HOLDING AND DECISION, relates to the CONCISE RULE OF LAW behind the decision)
- HR (HOLDING AND DECISION, gives the RATIONALE or reasoning behind the decision)
- HA (HOLDING AND DECISION, APPLIES the general principle(s) of law to the facts of the case to arrive at the decision)

Remember that a particular passage may well contain information necessary to more than one part of your brief, in which case you simply note that in the margin. If you are using the color-coded underlining method instead of margin notation, simply make asterisks or checks in the margin next to the passage in question in the colors that indicate the additional sections of the brief where it might be utilized.

The economy of utilizing "shorthand" in marking cases for briefing can be maintained in the actual brief writing process itself by utilizing "law student shorthand" within the brief. There are many commonly used words and phrases for which abbreviations can be substituted in your briefs (and in your class notes also). You can develop abbreviations that are personal to you and which will save you a lot of time. A reference list of briefing abbreviations will be found elsewhere in this book.

C. USE BOTH THE BRIEFING PROCESS AND THE BRIEF AS A LEARNING TOOL

Now that you have a format and the tools for briefing cases efficiently, the most important thing is to make the time spent in briefing profitable to you and to make the most advantageous use of the briefs you create. Of course, the briefs are invaluable for classroom reference when you are called upon to explain or analyze a particular case. However, they are also useful in reviewing for exams. A quick glance at the fact summary should bring the case to mind, and a rereading of the concise rule of law should enable you to go over the underlying legal concept in your mind, how it was applied in that particular case, and how it might apply in other factual settings.

As to the value to be derived from engaging in the briefing process itself, there is an immediate benefit that arises from being forced to sift through the essential facts and reasoning from the court's opinion and to succinctly express them in your own words in your brief. The process ensures that you understand the case and the point that it illustrates, and that means you will be ready to absorb further analysis and information brought forth in class. It also ensures you will have something to say when called upon in class. The briefing process helps develop a mental agility for getting to the *gist* of a case and for identifying, expounding on, and applying the legal concepts and issues found there. Of most immediate concern, that is the mental process on which you must rely in taking law school examinations. Of more asting concern, it is also the mental process upon which a lawyer relies in serving his clients and in making his living.

Notes

GLOSSARY

COMMON LATIN WORDS AND PHRASES ENCOUNTERED IN LAW

A FORTIORI: Because one fact exists or has been proven, therefore a second fact that is related to the first fact must also exist.

A PRIORI: From the cause to the effect. A term of logic used to denote that when one generally accepted truth is shown to be a cause, another particular effect must necessarily follow.

AB INITIO: From the beginning; a condition which has existed throughout, as in a marriage which was void ab initio.

ACTUS REUS: The wrongful act; in criminal law, such action sufficient to trigger criminal liability.

AD VALOREM: According to value; an ad valorem tax is imposed upon an item located within the taxing jurisdiction calculated by the value of such item.

AMICUS CURIAE: Friend of the court. Its most common usage takes the form of an amicus curiae brief, filed by a person who is not a party to an action but is nonetheless allowed to offer an argument supporting his legal interests.

ARGUENDO: In arguing. A statement, possibly hypothetical, made for the purpose of argument, is one made arguendo.

BILL QUIA TIMET: A bill to quiet title (establish ownership) to real property.

BONA FIDE: True, honest, or genuine. May refer to a person's legal position based on good faith or lacking notice of fraud (such as a bona fide purchaser for value) or to the authenticity of a particular document (such as a bona fide last will and testament).

CAUSA MORTIS: With approaching death in mind. A gift causa mortis is a gift given by a party who feels certain that death is imminent.

CAVEAT EMPTOR: Let the buyer beware. This maxim is reflected in the rule of law that a buyer purchases at his own risk because it is his responsibility to examine, judge, test, and otherwise inspect what he is buying.

CERTIORARI: A writ of review. Petitions for review of a case by the United States Supreme Court are most often done by means of a writ of certiorari.

CONTRA: On the other hand. Opposite. Contrary to.

CORAM NOBIS: Before us; writs of error directed to the court that originally rendered the judgment.

CORAM VOBIS: Before you; writs of error directed by an appellate court to a lower court to correct a factual error.

CORPUS DELICTI: The body of the crime; the requisite elements of a crime amounting to objective proof that a crime has been committed.

CUM TESTAMENTO ANNEXO, ADMINISTRATOR (ADMINISTRATOR C.T.A.): With will annexed; an administrator c.t.a. settles an estate pursuant to a will in which he is not appointed.

DE BONIS NON, ADMINISTRATOR (ADMINISTRATOR D.B.N.): Of goods not administered; an administrator d.b.n. settles a partially settled estate.

DE FACTO: In fact; in reality; actually. Existing in fact but not officially approved or engendered.

DE JURE: By right; lawful. Describes a condition that is legitimate "as a matter of law," in contrast to the term "de facto," which connotes something existing in fact but not legally sanctioned or authorized. For example, de facto segregation refers to segregation brought about by housing patterns, etc., whereas de jure segregation refers to segregation created by law.

DE MINIMUS: Of minimal importance; insignificant; a trifle; not worth bothering about.

DE NOVO: Anew; a second time; afresh. A trial de novo is a new trial held at the appellate level as if the case originated there and the trial at a lower level had not taken place.

DICTA: Generally used as an abbreviated form of obiter dicta, a term describing those portions of a judicial opinion incidental or not necessary to resolution of the specific question before the court. Such nonessential statements and remarks are not considered to be binding precedent.

DUCES TECUM: Refers to a particular type of writ or subpoena requesting a party or organization to produce certain documents in their possession.

EN BANC: Full bench. Where a court sits with all justices present rather than the usual quorum.

EX PARTE: For one side or one party only. An ex parte proceeding is one undertaken for the benefit of only one party, without notice to, or an appearance by, an adverse party.

EX POST FACTO: After the fact. An ex post facto law is a law that retroactively changes the consequences of a prior act.

EX REL.: Abbreviated form of the term ex relatione, meaning, upon relation or information. When the state brings an action in which it has no interest against an individual at the instigation of one who has a private interest in the matter.

FORUM NON CONVENIENS: Inconvenient forum. Although a court may have jurisdiction over the case, the action should be tried in a more conveniently located court, one to which parties and witnesses may more easily travel, for example.

GUARDIAN AD LITEM: A guardian of an infant as to litigation, appointed to represent the infant and pursue his/her rights.

HABEAS CORPUS: You have the body. The modern writ of habeas corpus is a writ directing that a person (body) being detained (such as a prisoner) be brought before the court so that the legality of his detention can be judicially ascertained.

IN CAMERA: In private, in chambers. When a hearing is held before a judge in his chambers or when all spectators are excluded from the courtroom.

IN FORMA PAUPERIS: In the manner of a pauper. A party who proceeds in forma pauperis because of his poverty is one who is allowed to bring suit without liability for costs.

INFRA: Below, under. A word referring the reader to a later part of a book. (The opposite of supra.)

IN LOCO PARENTIS: In the place of a parent.

IN PARI DELICTO: Equally wrong; a court of equity will not grant requested relief to an applicant who is in pari delicto, or as much at fault in the transactions giving rise to the controversy as is the opponent of the applicant.

IN PARI MATERIA: On like subject matter or upon the same matter. Statutes relating to the same person or things are said to be in pari materia. It is a general rule of statutory construction that such statutes should be construed together, i.e., looked at as if they together constituted one law.

IN PERSONAM: Against the person. Jurisdiction over the person of an individual.

IN RE: In the matter of. Used to designate a proceeding involving an estate or other property.

IN REM: A term that signifies an action against the res, or thing. An action in rem is basically one that is taken directly against property, as distinguished from an action in personam, i.e., against the person.

INTER ALIA: Among other things. Used to show that the whole of a statement, pleading, list, statute, etc., has not been set forth in its entirety.

INTER PARTES: Between the parties. May refer to contracts, conveyances or other transactions having legal significance.

INTER VIVOS: Between the living. An inter vivos gift is a gift made by a living grantor, as distinguished from bequests contained in a will, which pass upon the death of the testator.

IPSO FACTO: By the mere fact itself.

JUS: Law or the entire body of law.

LEX LOCI: The law of the place; the notion that the rights of parties to a legal proceeding are governed by the law of the place where those rights arose.

MALUM IN SE: Evil or wrong in and of itself; inherently wrong. This term describes an act that is wrong by its very nature, as opposed to one which would not be wrong but for the fact that there is a specific legal prohibition against it (malum prohibitum).

MALUM PROHIBITUM: Wrong because prohibited, but not inherently evil. Used to describe something that is wrong because it is expressly forbidden by law but that is not in and of itself evil, e.g., speeding.

MANDAMUS: We command. A writ directing an official to take a certain action.

MENS REA: A guilty mind; a criminal intent. A term used to signify the mental state that accompanies a crime or other prohibited act. Some crimes require only a general mens rea (general intent to do the prohibited act), but others, like assault with intent to murder, require the existence of a specific mens rea.

MODUS OPERANDI: Method of operating; generally refers to the manner or style of a criminal in committing crimes, admissible in appropriate cases as evidence of the identity of a defendant.

NEXUS: A connection to.

NISI PRIUS: A court of first impression. A nisi prius court is one where issues of fact are tried before a judge or jury.

N.O.V. (NON OBSTANTE VEREDICTO): Notwithstanding the verdict. A judgment n.o.v. is a judgment given in favor of one party despite the fact that a verdict was returned in favor of the other party, the justification being that the verdict either had no reasonable support in fact or was contrary to law.

NUNC PRO TUNC: Now for then. This phrase refers to actions that may be taken and will then have full retroactive effect.

PENDENTE LITE: Pending the suit; pending litigation underway.

PER CAPITA: By head; beneficiaries of an estate, if they take in equal shares, take per capita.

PER CURIAM: By the court; signifies an opinion ostensibly written "by the whole court" and with no identified author.

PER SE: By itself, in itself; inherently.

PER STIRPES: By representation. Used primarily in the law of wills to describe the method of distribution where a person, generally because of death, is unable to take that which is left to him by the will of another, and therefore his heirs divide such property between them rather than take under the will individually.

PRIMA FACIE: On its face, at first sight. A prima facie case is one that is sufficient on its face, meaning that the evidence supporting it is adequate to establish the case until contradicted or overcome by other evidence.

PRO TANTO: For so much; as far as it goes. Often used in eminent domain cases when a property owner receives partial payment for his land without prejudice to his right to bring suit for the full amount he claims his land to be worth.

QUANTUM MERUIT: As much as he deserves. Refers to recovery based on the doctrine of unjust enrichment in those cases in which a party has rendered valuable services or furnished materials that were accepted and enjoyed by another under circumstances that would reasonably notify the recipient that the rendering party expected to be paid. In essence, the law implies a contract to pay the reasonable value of the services or materials furnished.

QUASI: Almost like; as if; nearly. This term is essentially used to signify that one subject or thing is almost analogous to another but that material differences between them do exist. For example, a quasi-criminal proceeding is one that is not strictly criminal but shares enough of the same characteristics to require some of the same safeguards (e.g., procedural due process must be followed in a parol hearing).

QUID PRO QUO: Something for something. In contract law, the consideration, something of value, passed between the parties to render the contract binding.

RES GESTAE: Things done; in evidence law, this principle justifies the admission of a statement that would otherwise be hearsay when it is made so closely to the event in question as to be said to be a part of it, or with such spontaneity as not to have the possibility of falsehood.

RES IPSA LOQUITUR: The thing speaks for itself. This doctrine gives rise to a rebuttable presumption of negligence when the instrumentality causing the injury was within the exclusive control of the defendant, and the injury was one that does not normally occur unless a person has been negligent.

RES JUDICATA: A matter adjudged. Doctrine which provides that once a court of competent jurisdiction has rendered a final judgment or decree on the merits, that judgment or decree is conclusive upon the parties to the case and prevents them from engaging in any other litigation on the points and issues determined therein.

RESPONDEAT SUPERIOR: Let the master reply. This doctrine holds the master liable for the wrongful acts of his servant (or the principal for his agent) in those cases in which the servant (or agent) was acting within the scope of his authority at the time of the injury.

STARE DECISIS: To stand by or adhere to that which has been decided. The common law doctrine of stare decisis attempts to give security and certainty to the law by following the policy that once a principle of law as applicable to a certain set of facts has been set forth in a decision, it forms a precedent which will subsequently be followed, even though a different decision might be made were it the first time the question had arisen. Of course, stare decisis is not an inviolable principle and is departed from in instances where there is good cause (e.g., considerations of public policy led the Supreme Court to disregard prior decisions sanctioning segregation).

SUPRA: Above. A word referring a reader to an earlier part of a book.

ULTRA VIRES: Beyond the power. This phrase is most commonly used to refer to actions taken by a corporation that are beyond the power or legal authority of the corporation.

ADDENDUM OF FRENCH DERIVATIVES

IN PAIS: Not pursuant to legal proceedings.

CHATTEL: Tangible personal property.

CY PRES: Doctrine permitting courts to apply trust funds to purposes not expressed in the trust but necessary to carry out the settlor's intent.

PER AUTRE VIE: For another's life; in property law, an estate may be granted that will terminate upon the death of someone other than the grantee.

PROFIT A PRENDRE: A license to remove minerals or other produce from land.

VOIR DIRE: Process of questioning jurors as to their predispositions about the case or parties to a proceeding in order to identify those jurors displaying bias or prejudice.

Notes

TABLE OF CASES

A
Argersinger v. Hamlin 10
Arizona v. Fulminante 111
Ash, United States v., ... 27

B
Baltimore City Dept. of Social Services v. Bouknight 87
Bearden v. Georgia 14
Boyd v. United States 31
Bram v. United States 88
Braswell v. United States 35
Brewer v. Williams 98
Brown v. Walker 81

C
California v. Acevedo 51
California v. Byers 85
California v. Hodari, D. 44
Camara v. Municipal Court of San Francisco 53
Caplin & Drysdale, Chartered v. United States 21
Ceccolini v. United States 69
Chambers v. Maroney 50
Chimel v. California 55
Colorado v. Bertine 58
Colorado v. Connelly 103
Crews v. United States 70
Cuyler v. Sullivan 18

D
Davis v. United States 97
DeCoster, United States v. 16
Delaware v. Prouse 59
Doe v. United States 34, 84
Duncan v. Louisiana 3

E
Evitts v. Lucey 13

F
Faretta v. California 19
Florida v. Riley 43

G
Gideon v. Wainwright 9
Griffith v. Kentucky 5

H
Harrington v. California 110
Harris v. New York 108
Haven, United States v. 109

I
Illinois v. Gates 48
Illinois v. Perkins 94

J
Jacobson v. United States 75

K
Kastigar v. United States 83
Katz v. United States 41
Kirby v. Illinois 26

L
Leon, United States v. 71

M
Manson v. Brathwaite 28
Mapp v. Ohio 46
Massiah v. United States 89
McKaskle v. Wiggins 20
McNeil v. Wisconsin 100
Medina v. California 4
Michigan v. Jackson 99
Michigan v. Summers 62
Michigan Dept. of State Police v. Sitz 60
Minnesota v. Murphy 93
Miranda v. Arizona 90
Moran v. Burbine 95

N
New York v. Belton 57
New York v. Class 63
New York v. Quarles 101
Nix v. Whiteside 17
Nix v. Williams 112

O
Oregon v. Bradshaw 96
Oregon v. Elstad 102

P
Payner, United States v. 76
Payton v. New York 52
Pennsylvania v. Muniz 92

R
Rakas v. Illinois 67
Rawlings v. Kentucky 68
Rhode Island v. Innis 91
Robinson, United States v. 56
Ross v. Moffitt 12

Continued on next page

Notes

TABLE OF CASES (Continued)

S
Schmerber v. California 32
Schneckloth v. Bustamonte 66
Scott v. Illinois 11
South Dakota v. Neville 86
Spinelli v. United States 47
Strickland v. Washington 15

T
Teague v. Lane 6
Tennessee v. Garner 65
Terry v. Ohio 54

U
Ullmann v. United States 82

W
Wade, United States v., ... 25
Walder v. United States 107
Warden, Maryland Penitentiary v. Hayden 33, 49
White, United States v., ... 42
Wolf v. Colorado 45

Y
Ybarra v. Illinois 61

Z
Zurcher v. Stanford Daily 64

CASENOTE LEGAL BRIEFS —CRIMINAL PROCEDURE

CHAPTER 3*
THE PROCESS OF CONSTITUTIONAL DECISIONMAKING

QUICK REFERENCE RULES OF LAW

1. **Constitutional Decisionmaking.** States must provide a defendant in a nonpetty criminal proceeding the right to trial by jury. (Duncan v. Louisiana)

2. **Incorporation of the Bill of Rights.** A state may constitutionally place the burden of proof on a criminal defendant raising incompetency as an issue. (Medina v. California)

    [For more information on incorporation of Bill of Rights, see Casenote Law Outline on Criminal Procedure, Chapter 1, § III.]

3. **Retroactivity.** A Supreme Court decision announcing a new constitutional standard of criminal procedure will be applied retroactively to all cases on direct appeal, even if the new rule represents a clear break with precedent. (Griffith v. Kentucky)

4. **Retroactivity.** Except in special circumstances, case law will not be retroactively applied in collateral review. (Teague v. Lane)

---

* There are no cases in Chapters 1 & 2.

NOTES

DUNCAN v. LOUISIANA
391 U.S. 195 (1968).

NATURE OF CASE: Review of conviction of battery.

FACT SUMMARY: Duncan (D), convicted of battery after a court trial, contended that he was constitutionally entitled to a jury trial.

CONCISE RULE OF LAW: States must provide a defendant in a nonpetty criminal proceeding the right to trial by jury.

FACTS: Duncan (D) was charged with simple battery, an offense with a maximum penalty of two years in state penitentiary. He requested a jury trial but was denied same. Convicted by a court, he was sentenced to 60 days in a parish (county) jail. The Louisiana Supreme Court upheld the conviction, and the U.S. Supreme Court granted review.

ISSUE: Must states provide a defendant in a nonpetty criminal proceeding the right to trial by jury?

HOLDING AND DECISION: (White, J.) Yes. States must provide a defendant in a nonpetty criminal proceeding the right to trial by jury. The Fourteenth Amendment imposes upon states the obligation not to deny due process of law to their citizens. Increasingly, the rights enumerated in the first eight amendments have been incorporated into the Fourteenth Amendment's Due Process Clause. Whether such incorporation is appropriate depends upon whether the right at issue is fundamental to liberty and basic to our system of jurisprudence. It is this Court's judgment that the Sixth Amendment's right to trial by jury is such a right. Jury trials exist in criminal cases to protect citizens from corrupt or incompetent prosecutors and biased or unfair judges. Despite its flaws, the jury system has become so central to the American notion of liberty that it cannot be said that due process can exist without it. Consequently, the Fourteenth Amendment requires that any nonpetty offense prosecution afford the right to trial by jury. Here, the charged offense carried a penalty of up to two years' imprisonment and, hence, cannot be called petty. Therefore, Duncan (D) was entitled to a jury trial. Reversed.

CONCURRENCE: (Black, J.) The Fourteenth Amendment incorporated in its Due Process Clause all rights enumerated in the Bill of Rights.

DISSENT: (Harlan, J.) The Due Process Clause only requires that criminal trials be fundamentally fair; it does not impose upon states any particular requirement as to how they must make them fair.

EDITOR'S ANALYSIS: The extent to which the Fourteenth Amendment's Due Process Clause incorporates the Bill of Rights is an old one. Some Supreme Court jurists, most notably Justice Black, called for 100% incorporation. This has never been fully done, although most of the Bill of Rights have in fact been incorporated. On the other hand, the Court has read into the Clause rights not found in the Bill of Rights, most notably privacy.

NOTES:

MEDINA v. CALIFORNIA
___U.S.___, 112 S. Ct. 2572 (1992).

NATURE OF CASE: Review of criminal conviction.

FACT SUMMARY: Medina (D), a criminal defendant, contended that a California law that required him to prove his incompetency to stand trial violated due process.

CONCISE RULE OF LAW: A state may constitutionally place the burden of proof on a criminal defendant raising incompetency as an issue.

FACTS: Medina (D) was criminally charged. He raised the issue of competence to stand trial. A hearing was held on the matter. California law placed the burden of proof on the defendant to prove incompetency by a preponderance of evidence. Medina (D) failed to carry that burden and was held to be competent to stand trial. He was convicted and appealed, contending that placing the burden of proving incompetency upon him violated due process. He argued that, to determine the allocation of the burden of proof, the court should have applied the test enunciated in Mathews v. Eldridge, 424 U.S. 319 (1976), whereby the deprivation of an individual's private interest is weighed against administrative efficiency.

ISSUE: May a state constitutionally place the burden of proof on a defendant raising incompetency as an issue?

HOLDING AND DECISION: (Kennedy, J.) Yes. A state may constitutionally place the burden of proof on a defendant raising incompetency as an issue. In the realm of criminal procedure, the states have, in most cases, more experience and expertise than the federal government. For that reason, only those state procedures that violate a narrowly defined concept of fundamental fairness will be held to violate due process. The Bill of Rights, as incorporated into the Fourteenth Amendment, largely sets the limits on state procedural powers. A state procedure not prohibited by the Bill of Rights will be held to violate due process only if it offends some principle of justice so rooted in the traditions and conscience of our people as to be ranked as fundamental. In the context of this case, there is no settled tradition on the proper allocation of burden of proof in a competency hearing. Consequently, California's burden of proof does not offend due process. Affirmed.

CONCURRENCE: (O'Connor, J.) The balancing of equities test of Mathews v. Eldridge may be appropriate in a due process evaluation of a state criminal procedure.

DISSENT: (Blackmun, J.) A Constitution that forbids the trial of an incompetent person should not tolerate such a trial when the evidence of competency is equivocal.

EDITOR'S ANALYSIS: The Court has created very different tests for evaluating due process in the civil and criminal arenas. The test for the criminal context is described in the above case. The civil framework fashioned in Mathews v. Eldridge, which is considerably less deferential, involves a three-part test: the court must consider (1) the private interest that will be affected by the official action; (2) the risk of an erroneous deprivation of such interest and the value of additional procedural safeguards; and (3) the government's interest, including the fiscal burdens that additional procedural safeguards would entail.

[For more information on incorporation of Bill of Rights, see Casenote Law Outline on Criminal Procedure, Chapter 1, § III.]

NOTES:

GRIFFITH v. KENTUCKY
479 U.S. 314 (1987).

NATURE OF CASE: Review of robbery conviction.

FACT SUMMARY: The state of Kentucky (P) argued that a Supreme Court decision forcing prosecutors to justify race-based jury selection should be applied to Griffith's (D) pending appeal because it represented a clear break with precedent.

CONCISE RULE OF LAW: A Supreme Court decision announcing a new constitutional standard of criminal procedure will be applied retroactively to all cases on direct appeal, even if the new rule represents a clear break with precedent.

FACTS: During Griffith's (D) robbery trial, the prosecution used peremptory challenges to empanel an all-white jury. Griffith (D), who was black, was convicted. While his case was on appeal, the Supreme Court decided Batson v. Kentucky, 476 U.S. 79 (1986), which held that the use of race-conscious peremptory challenges was unconstitutional. The Kentucky Supreme Court declined to give retroactive effect to Batson, as it represented a clear break with precedent, and therefore affirmed Griffith's (D) conviction. The Supreme Court granted review.

ISSUE: Will a Supreme Court decision announcing a new standard of criminal procedure be applied retroactively to all cases on direct appeal, even if the new rule represents a clear break with precedent?

HOLDING AND DECISION: (Blackmun, J.) Yes. A Supreme Court decision will be applied retroactively to all cases on direct appeal, even if it represents a clear break with precedent. Failure to apply a newly declared constitutional rule to criminal cases pending on direct review violates basic norms of constitutional adjudication. The integrity of judicial review requires that a rule be applied to all similar cases pending on direct review. This is a necessary corollary to the basic principle of treating similarly situated defendants the same. to exclude retroactivity in some cases but not others violates this principle. These considerations, this Court believes, outweigh a state's interest in settled adjudications. Reversed.

CONCURRENCE: (Powell, J.) The rule announced here today should not apply to habeas corpus petitions.

DISSENT: (Rehnquist, J.) New constitutional rules governing criminal prosecutions should apply retroactively to cases pending on direct appeal when the rule is announced but, with narrow exceptions, should not apply in collateral proceedings challenging final convictions.

DISSENT: (White, J.) Why retroactivity is to be treated differently in direct review and collateral review is analytically unclear.

EDITOR'S ANALYSIS: As Justice White's dissent notes, the Court has treated retroactivity quite differently in collateral review as opposed to direct appeal. In Allen v. Hardy, 478 U.S. 255 (1986), the court refused to retroactively apply Batson to habeas actions. This represents a relatively new approach. In earlier cases, such as Stovall v. Denno, 388 U.S. 293 (1967), the Court treated habeas and direct review in the same manner.

NOTES:

TEAGUE v. LANE
489 U.S. 288 (1989).

NATURE OF CASE: Review of denial of habeas corpus.

FACT SUMMARY: Teague (D) argued in a habeas proceeding that a post-conviction judicial decision had rendered his conviction invalid.

CONCISE RULE OF LAW: Except in special circumstances, case law will not be retroactively applied in collateral review.

FACTS: Teague (D) was charged with various felonies. An all-white jury convicted Teague (D), a black man, of attempted murder, robbery, and battery. The prosecution had used all its peremptory challenges to exclude blacks from the jury. Teague (D) appealed, contending that this denied him due process. On appeal the conviction was upheld. Teague (D) subsequently petitioned for habeas corpus, contending that he had been entitled to a jury consisting of a cross-section of the community. The district court denied his petition on the merits, as did the court of appeals. The Supreme Court granted review.

ISSUE: Will case law be retroactively applied in collateral review?

HOLDING AND DECISION: (O'Connor, J.) No. Case law will not be retroactively applied in collateral review. Habeas corpus provides an avenue for upsetting judgments that otherwise would be final. It is not intended to be a substitute for direct review. Both the state and criminal defendants have an interest in leaving concluded litigation in a state of repose. If new rules of constitutional law were to be applied retroactively, any litigation might be reopened if the new rule were to be applicable. Further, the purpose of habeas is that its presence creates an incentive for trial and appellate judges to conduct their proceedings in a manner consistent with established constitutional principles. To apply new principles retroactively would actually subvert this purpose. Therefore, the Court concludes that, unless the post-conviction rule announced is so fundamental to the concept of ordered liberty that it would be unconscionable not to retroactively apply it, retroactive application will not be given. A necessary corollary to this rule is that no new rule of constitutional criminal procedure should be announced in a habeas proceeding. Here, to rule as Teague (D) urges would amount to that. Therefore, without ruling on the merits of the claim, the denial of habeas must be affirmed.

CONCURRENCE: (White, J.) The proper test for retroactivity should be whether the matter is on direct or collateral review, weighing of the purpose of the new rule, the extent of reliance on the old rule, and retroactivity's effect on the administration of justice.

CONCURRENCE: (Stevens, J.) The test adopted by the Court is essentially proper. However, as to the Court's discussion of the "fundamental fairness" exception, the Court gives an excessively result-oriented analysis.

DISSENT: (Brennan, J.) Permitting the federal courts to decide novel habeas claims not substantially related to guilt or innocence has profited our society immensely. In the face of congressional acquiescence to this practice, it is ill-advised for the Court to now fashion such a major change in habeas jurisprudence.

EDITOR'S ANALYSIS: The opinion in fact announces two rules, the first being that stated above and the second being that new constitutional issues cannot be announced in a habeas proceeding. The latter rule is potentially much more significant than the first. It is important to note, however, that only four justices joined the section announcing that rule, which limits its precedential value.

NOTES:

CHAPTER 4
THE RIGHT TO COUNSEL AND OTHER ASSISTANCE

QUICK REFERENCE RULES OF LAW

1. **Right to Appointed Counsel at Trial.** The right of an indigent to appointed counsel is a right fundamental and essential to a fair trial. (Gideon v. Wainwright)

   [For more information on right to appointed counsel at trial, see Casenote Law Outline on Criminal Procedure, Chapter 17, § I, Right to Appointed Counsel at Trial.]

2. **Right to Appointed Counsel at Trial.** Absent a knowing and intelligent waiver, no person may be imprisoned for any offense unless he is represented by counsel. (Argersinger v. Hamlin)

   [For more information on right to appointed counsel at trial, see Casenote Law Outline on Criminal Procedure, Chapter 17, § I, Right to Appointed Counsel at Trial.]

3. **Right to Appointed Counsel at Trial.** The Constitution does not guarantee a right to counsel to a person charged in state court with a misdemeanor punishable by imprisonment, unless a prison term actually is imposed. (Scott v. Illinois)

   [For more information on right to appointed counsel at trial, see Casenote Law Outline on Criminal Procedure, Chapter 17, § I, Right to Appointed Counsel at Trial.]

4. **Right to Appointed Counsel on Appeal.** An indigent defendant is not entitled to court-appointed counsel to handle a discretionary appeal. (Ross v. Moffitt)

   [For more information on right to counsel on appeal, see Casenote Law Outline on Criminal Procedure, Chapter 17, § III, Right to Appointed Counsel on Appeal.]

5. **Right to Counsel on Appeal.** An indigent defendant in an appeal as of right is entitled to effective assistance of counsel. (Evitts v. Lucey)

   [For more information on right to counsel on appeal, see Casenote Law Outline on Criminal Procedure, Chapter 17, § III, Right to Appointed Counsel on Appeal.]

6. **Failure to Pay Restitution.** A court may not automatically revoke probation when a convict stops paying a fine on account of indigence. (Bearden v. Georgia)

7. **Adequate Representation.** At a capital sentence hearing, a Sixth Amendment violation occurs only if counsel's performance was deficient and such deficiency resulted in actual prejudice. (Strickland v. Washington)

   [For more information on adequate representation, see Casenote Law Outline on Criminal Procedure, Chapter 17, § IV, Right to Effective Representation of Counsel.]

8. **Effective Assistance of Counsel.** A defendant is not denied effective assistance of counsel if his attorney dissuades him from committing perjury. (Nix v. Whiteside)

9. **Effective Assistance of Counsel.** (1) A state trial judge is under no duty to inquire into the propriety of multiple representation, absent objection. (2) The mere possibility of a conflict of interest does not create a Sixth Amendment violation. (Cuyler v. Sullivan)

10. **The Right to Control the Lawyering Process.** A state may not constitutionally impose a lawyer on a defendant who wishes to represent himself, so long as the defendant has made a knowing and intelligent waiver of his right to a lawyer. (Faretta v. California)

11. **Self-Representation.** Standby counsel to a pro se criminal defendant does not commit a Sixth Amendment violation by failing to remain silent. (McKaskle v. Wiggins)

    [For more information on self-representation, see Casenote Law Outline on Criminal Procedure, Chapter 17, § II, Right to Self-Representation at Trial.]

12. **The Implications of Forfeiture Statutes.** A forfeiture statute is not unconstitutional because it prevents a defendant from obtaining private counsel. (Caplin & Drysdale, Chartered v. United States)

GIDEON v. WAINWRIGHT
372 U.S. 335 (1963).

NATURE OF CASE: Felony prosecution.

FACT SUMMARY: Gideon (D) was charged with a felony in a state prosecution. He requested court-appointed counsel, but was refused on the basis state law only required appointment of counsel in capital cases.

CONCISE RULE OF LAW: The right of an indigent to appointed counsel is a right fundamental and essential to a fair trial.

FACTS: Gideon (D) was charged with felony breaking and entering, a violation of state law. He was without funds and requested the court to appoint an attorney for him at trial. The request was refused since the state law did not require appointment of counsel for indigents except in capital offense cases. Gideon then conducted his own defense and was convicted and sentenced to five years. He filed a writ of habeas corpus based on the denial of counsel at trial.

ISSUE: Is the right to the assistance of counsel at trial a fundamental and essential right required to insure a fair trial?

HOLDING AND DECISION: (Black, J.) Yes. This Court first expressed the view that the right to counsel at trial was a fundamental right essential to a fair trial in Powell v. Alabama. That decision was limited to its facts, however. In Betts v. Brady, the right to counsel was predicated on a case-by-case examination of the special circumstances of each case to determine if denial of counsel was a denial of a fair trial. But it is evident that every defendant who can afford a lawyer will have one at his criminal trial. It does not appear to be a luxury but is viewed as a necessity. This Court is of the opinion, now, that Powell v. Alabama was right in holding that the right to counsel is fundamental to a fair trial and that Betts v. Brady was wrong in limiting that right to special circumstances. The Court holds that the right to counsel is a fundamental right for all criminal defendants at trial.

CONCURRENCE: (Douglas, J.) First, the Fourteenth Amendment should be understood as incorporating the entire Bill of Rights. Second, as the Court has held, rights protected against state invasion by the Due Process Clause of the Fourteenth Amendment are equal versions of what the Bill of Rights protects against federal invasion.

CONCURRENCE: (Clark, J.) The Sixth Amendment guarantees a right to counsel in all federal criminal cases, and prior Court decisions have recognized a Fourteenth Amendment right to counsel in state capital cases. This case extends the right to counsel to all state criminal cases, erasing a distinction between capital and noncapital cases having no basis in the Constitution. The Constitution requires due process of law for deprivations of "life" and "liberty," and constitutionally, there cannot be a difference in the quality of the process.

CONCURRENCE: (Harlan, J.) Under the "special circumstances" rule, the Fourteenth Amendment has not been considered to guarantee a right to counsel in all state criminal cases but only where presence of counsel is a necessary requisite of due process. The special circumstances rule has been eliminated in state capital cases and has been steadily eroded in noncapital cases. The Court has recognized that the mere existence of a serious criminal charge carrying the possibility of a substantial prison sentence constitutes special circumstances requiring presence of counsel. However, this decision should not be read to "incorporate" the Sixth Amendment into the Fourteenth. A Sixth Amendment right to counsel and a Fourteenth Amendment right to counsel may mean different things, considering the different legitimate interests of federal and state governments.

EDITOR'S ANALYSIS: Upon retrial, with the assistance of appointed counsel, Gideon was acquitted. The Gideon decision was read to require counsel in only non-petty (i.e., six months or more imprisonment) cases. However, in a subsequent case, Argersinger v. Hamlin, the right to appointed counsel was extended to any case where the possibility of imprisonment existed. There was no minimum time specified and so if the judge wishes to imprison the defendant, if convicted, he must have appointed counsel, if indigent. The denial of counsel at trial where imprisonment results is error per se not subject to the harmless error rule.

[For more information on right to appointed counsel at trial, see Casenote Law Outline on Criminal Procedure, Chapter 17, § I, Right to Appointed Counsel at Trial.]

NOTES:

ARGERSINGER v. HAMLIN
407 U.S. 25 (1972).

NATURE OF CASE: Constitutional challenge against the denial of appointed counsel in misdemeanor cases.

FACT SUMMARY: Argersinger (P) was convicted of a misdemeanor and was sentenced to 90 days in jail after being denied court-appointed counsel.

CONCISE RULE OF LAW: Absent a knowing and intelligent waiver, no person may be imprisoned for any offense unless he is represented by counsel.

FACTS: Argersinger (P) was charged with carrying a concealed weapon. This was a misdemeanor in Florida, punishable by up to six months in prison, a fine of $1,000, or both. Argersinger (P), an indigent, requested appointed counsel. The court denied the request, since the charge was a misdemeanor. Argersinger (P) was convicted and sentenced to 90 days in jail. Argersinger's (P) habeas corpus petition was denied by the Florida Supreme Court on the issue of whether the denial of court-appointed counsel in misdemeanor cases involving jail sentences violated the Fourteenth Amendment's Due Process Clause.

ISSUE: Does the denial of court-appointed counsel in misdemeanor cases involving jail sentences violate the Due Process Clause of the Fourteenth Amendment?

HOLDING AND DECISION: (Douglas, J.) Yes. The legal questions involved in misdemeanor cases are no less complex than in felony cases. Similar skill and knowledge is required in both types of cases to present an adequate defense. Moreover, there is a tendency to process misdemeanor cases in an assembly-line manner which often results in a denial of justice. A study by the American Civil Liberties Union shows that a party accused of a misdemeanor and who has counsel is five times as likely to have the charges dismissed as is the accused who is not represented by counsel. An attorney is therefore often required to assure a fair trial. We conclude that the denial of a court-appointed attorney in misdemeanor cases involving a jail sentence violates the Due Process Clause of the Fourteenth Amendment unless the right is intelligently and knowingly waived. Reversed and remanded.

CONCURRENCE: (Brennan, J.) Law students as well as practicing attorneys may provide an important source of legal representation for the indigent. Given the large increase in law school enrollments, "I think it plain that law students can be looked to make a significant contribution, quantitatively and qualitatively, to the representation of the poor in many areas, including cases reached by today's decision."

CONCURRENCE: (Powell, J.) An accused's need of counsel does not disappear simply because the charged offense is punishable by less than six months in prison. A rule requiring appointment of counsel in all state criminal cases would have too great an adverse impact on administration of justice. The absolute, actual-imprisonment rule established by the majority is also too costly. A trial judge now must decide before trial, before hearing evidence, whether to appoint counsel or to forgo his discretion to impose imprisonment and abandon his legislatively-imposed duty to consider the full range of possible punishments. Due process does not require presence of counsel in all petty cases, only in cases where counsel is necessary to assure a fair trial. Many petty cases are exceedingly simple. Trial courts should be directed to determine the need for appointed counsel, considering the complexity of the offense, the seriousness of the probable sentence, and individual factors peculiar to the case, such as the competency of the defendant and the attitude of the community. This rule would be similar to the special-circumstances rule rejected for felony cases in Gideon. Applying this rule, refusal to appoint counsel in this case violated Argersinger's (D) right to due process.

EDITOR'S ANALYSIS: Counsel is required at all critical stages of criminal proceedings. There are a number of instances where counsel is not deemed necessary. For example, counsel is not required in parole revocation hearings, Morrissey v. Brewer, 408 U.S. 471 (1972), and in probation revocation proceedings, Gagnon v. Scarpelli, 411 U.S. 778 (1973). In certain cases, counsel is not required in pro-indictment police station identifications if in-court identifications have an independent basis. Kirby v. Illinois, 406 U.S. 682 (1972).

[For more information on right to appointed counsel at trial, see Casenote Law Outline on Criminal Procedure, Chapter 17, § I, Right to Appointed Counsel at Trial.]

NOTES:

SCOTT v. ILLINOIS
440 U.S. 367 (1979).

NATURE OF CASE: Appeal of theft conviction.

FACT SUMMARY: Without assistance of counsel, Scott (D) was convicted of misdemeanor theft, a crime carrying a possibility of one year of imprisonment, for which Scott (D) was fined $50.

CONCISE RULE OF LAW: The Constitution does not guarantee a right to counsel to a person charged in state court with a misdemeanor punishable by imprisonment, unless a prison term actually is imposed.

FACTS: Scott (D) was charged with misdemeanor theft, for which an Illinois statute set the penalty at up to a $500 fine and one year in prison. The trial court refused to appoint counsel to represent him. Scott (D) was convicted and fined $50 but received no prison term. Scott (D) appealed to the Illinois Supreme Court, claiming the Sixth and Fourteenth Amendments require appointment of counsel whenever imprisonment is an authorized penalty. (In Argersinger v. Hamlin, 407 U.S. 25 (1972), the Court held that a defendant charged with a "petty" offense has a right to counsel if he is sentenced to a term of imprisonment.) Scott's (D) conviction was upheld. Scott (D) appealed to the U.S. Supreme Court.

ISSUE: Does the Constitution guarantee a right to counsel to a person charged in state court with a misdemeanor punishable by imprisonment, where no prison term actually is imposed?

HOLDING AND DECISION: (Rehnquist, J.) No. The Constitution does not guarantee a right to counsel to a person charged in state court with a misdemeanor punishable by imprisonment, unless a prison term actually is imposed. The premise of Argersinger was that actual imprisonment is a more severe penalty than a fine or the mere threat of imprisonment, justifying actual imprisonment as the line defining right to counsel. This line has proven workable, whereas extension of right to counsel would create confusion and impose substantial costs on the states. Affirmed.

CONCURRENCE: (Powell, J.) The right to counsel should not be dependent on whether there is imprisonment. Drawing the line at imprisonment can have the practical effect of precluding the right to counsel in nonimprisonment cases where conviction can have more serious consequences. Moreover, a state trial judge must decide before trial, before hearing evidence, whether to appoint counsel or to forgo his discretion to impose imprisonment and abandon his legislatively imposed duty to consider the full range of possible punishments.

DISSENT: (Brennan, J.) Argersinger held that the right to counsel extends to "petty" offenses where actual imprisonment is imposed. The assumption in Argersinger was that the right to counsel also applies to all "nonpetty" offenses, i.e., offenses punishable by more than six months' imprisonment. This "authorized imprisonment" standard is a better predictor of whether the consequences of conviction are so serious that the Sixth Amendment requires appointment of counsel. An authorized imprisonment test also avoids forcing state judges to make pretrial choices between appointing counsel or forgoing the option of imposing imprisonment. The Court's concern that an authorized imprisonment rule would place a serious economic burden on the states should not serve to deny Constitutional rights. The Court's concern also is questionable in light of the proven economic feasibility of public defender systems and the fact that most states' laws currently mandate some form of an authorized imprisonment rule. The offense with which Scott (D) was charged, "theft," is certainly a "nonpetty" offense, carrying with it the moral stigma attached to common law crimes, as well as a possible one-year jail term. Scott (D) should have a right to counsel.

DISSENT: (Blackmun, J.) Right to counsel should extend to any case involving a "petty" offense, i.e., where the offense is punishable by more than six months' imprisonment, or to any "nonpetty" case where a prison term is actually imposed.

EDITOR'S ANALYSIS: The Court's opinion "adopt(s) actual imprisonment as the line defining the constitutional right to appointment of counsel." Scott (D) committed a misdemeanor, but neither the express words nor the logic of the opinion limit the holding to misdemeanors. Thus, it could be argued that after Scott indigents charged in state court with any crime, felony, or misdemeanor are not entitled to appointed counsel unless a prison term actually is imposed. However, the dominant interpretation is that Scott left the rule of Gideon intact: all felony defendants are entitled to appointed counsel.

[For more information on right to appointed counsel at trial, see Casenote Law Outline on Criminal Procedure, Chapter 17, § I, Right to Appointed Counsel at Trial.]

NOTES:

ROSS v. MOFFITT
417 U.S. 600 (1974).

NATURE OF CASE: Review of order granting writ of habeas corpus.

FACT SUMMARY: Moffitt (D) contended that he was entitled, due to his indigence, to court-appointed counsel to handle his petition for discretionary review of his criminal conviction.

CONCISE RULE OF LAW: An indigent defendant is not entitled to court-appointed counsel to handle a discretionary appeal.

FACTS: Moffitt (D) was convicted of a crime [not specified in the casebook opinion] in North Carolina state court. As an indigent, he was afforded court-appointed counsel, as he was on his appeal as of right to the state court of appeals, where his conviction was affirmed. For his petition for review in the North Carolina Supreme Court, he was not afforded counsel, and his petition was denied. He then petitioned for a writ of habeas corpus, contending that the failure to provide him with counsel in his petition for discretionary review violated his Sixth and Fourteenth Amendment right to counsel. The Fourth Circuit agreed and issued the writ. The Supreme Court granted review.

ISSUE: Is an indigent defendant entitled to court-appointed counsel to handle a discretionary appeal?

HOLDING AND DECISION: (Rehnquist, J.) No. An indigent defendant is not entitled to court-appointed counsel to handle a discretionary appeal. This Court has held that due process and/or equal protection entitles an indigent defendant to appointed counsel at trial and at appeals as of right. However, the right to counsel is not unlimited. With respect to due process, it has already been held that a state is not obligated to provide appellate review at all, so due process does not require counsel on appeal in any form. This Court has held that equal protection requires that an indigent defendant be given court-appointed counsel in an appeal as of right. However, a discretionary appeal is different. This type of appeal, generally made to a state supreme court or to this Court, does not involve issues of the petitioner's own guilt so much as broader issues of social policy. Since the petitioner's guilt is less directly implicated, equal protection issues fade in significance, so much so that court-appointed counsel is no longer required. The Fourth Circuit was therefore in error. Reversed.

DISSENT: (Douglas, J.) Permissive review is often the most meaningful review a convicted defendant will get, and the right to counsel is as powerful there as in a review as of right.

EDITOR'S ANALYSIS: The Supreme Court first took up the issue of an indigent's right to counsel in Griffin v. Illinois, 351 U.S. 12 (1956), in which it held that an indigent had a right to a free transcript in his appeal. Since then, the issue has been revisited in a number of contexts. The Court's most well-known foray into this issue was Gideon v. Wainwright, 372 U.S. 335 (1963), in which it held that an indigent was entitled to trial counsel.

[For more information on right to counsel on appeal, see Casenote Law Outline on Criminal Procedure, Chapter 17, § III, Right to Appointed Counsel on Appeal.]

NOTES:

EVITTS v. LUCEY
469 U.S. 387 (1985).

NATURE OF CASE: Review of grant of writ of habeas corpus.

FACT SUMMARY: Indigent Lucey (P) contended that in an appeal as of right his court-appointed attorney had been so incompetent that he had been denied effective counsel.

CONCISE RULE OF LAW: An indigent defendant in an appeal as of right is entitled to effective assistance of counsel.

FACTS: Lucey (P) was convicted in Kentucky state court of narcotics violations. An indigent, he was appointed counsel for an appeal as of right, to which he was entitled under state law. However, his attorney failed to follow certain procedures prescribed for appeals, and the appeal was dismissed. The Kentucky Supreme Court denied review. Lucey (P) then filed a federal habeas corpus petition, contending that he had not received effective assistance of counsel. The district court issued the writ, and the Sixth Circuit affirmed. The Supreme Court granted review.

ISSUE: Is an indigent defendant in an appeal as of right entitled to effective assistance of counsel?

HOLDING AND DECISION: (Brennan, J.) Yes. An indigent defendant in an appeal as of right is entitled to effective assistance of counsel. This Court has already held that, when a state affords an appeal as of right in criminal cases, an indigent defendant is entitled to court-appointed counsel. From this it necessarily flows that such counsel must be effective. An appeal is governed by rules too intricate for the layman, and due process requires that the defendant be afforded a realistic opportunity to employ the appellate process. Ineffective counsel is no better than no counsel at all. This Court has already held that appointed counsel at trial must be effective; the analysis is no different for appeals. The fact that a state is not obligated to provide appellate review is of no moment; having elected to provide one, a state must do so in a manner consistent with due process. Here, the courts below properly held Lucey (P) to have been denied effective assistance, and so his right to counsel was violated. Affirmed.

DISSENT: (Burger, C.J.) The Court has added yet another barrier to the finality of the appellate process.

DISSENT: (Rehnquist, J.) The Sixth Amendment provides a right to counsel in criminal prosecutions. The prosecution ends at conviction; the appellate process is an entirely different framework.

EDITOR'S ANALYSIS: In prior cases, the Court usually invoked equal protection as a basis for affording counsel to indigents. Here, it invoked the Due Process Clause. The two concepts are often used interchangeably, but they are distinct. Due process refers to relations between the state and the individual; equal protection refers to the state's treatment of different individuals.

[For more information on right to counsel on appeal, see Casenote Law Outline on Criminal Procedure, Chapter 17, § III, Right to Appointed Counsel on Appeal.]

NOTES:

BEARDEN v. GEORGIA
461 U.S. 660 (1983).

NATURE OF CASE: Review of sentencing determination.

FACT SUMMARY: Bearden (D), given a sentence of probation on condition of paying restitution, had his probation revoked when he became unable to pay.

CONCISE RULE OF LAW: A court may not automatically revoke probation when a convict stops paying a fine on account of indigence.

FACTS: Bearden (D) was convicted of burglary and receiving stolen property. As a first offender, he was given a sentence of probation on condition that he make restitution and pay a fine. Not long after receiving this sentence, he was laid off. Without work or savings, he was unable to pay. His probation was revoked, and he was ordered imprisoned. The Georgia court of appeals affirmed, and the Supreme Court granted review.

ISSUE: May a court automatically revoke probation when a convict stops paying a fine on account of indigence?

HOLDING AND DECISION: (O'Connor, J.) No. A court may not automatically revoke probation when a convict stops paying a fine on account of indigence. This Court has long been sensitive to the treatment of indigents by the criminal justice system. Using both due process and equal protection analyses, this Court has fashioned a general principle that a state may not treat indigents more harshly than other defendants solely on account of their indigence. In the context of this case, for a court to automatically revoke probation without having considered a defendant's ability to pay and the availability of alternative measures amounts to punishing him on account of his indigence. Rather, a sentencing court must make these inquiries in a revocation proceeding. Since such an inquiry was not made here, error occurred. Reversed.

DISSENT: (White, J.) Had the original sentencing court elected to imprison a defendant rather than order probation out of a concern for the defendant's inability to pay, no constitutional violation would have been available. From this it follows that a revocation for the same reason is likewise permissible.

EDITOR'S ANALYSIS: There are all sorts of situations where an indigent defendant is at a disadvantage vis-à-vis one with assets. Lower courts have long been trying to sort out the constitutional implications in such situations. For instance, it has been held that an indigent does not have a right to a court reporter. On the other hand, it has been held that a fee waiver for records retrieval is constitutionally mandated.

NOTES:

STRICKLAND v. WASHINGTON
466 U.S. 669 (1984).

NATURE OF CASE: Review of order granting writ of habeas corpus.

FACT SUMMARY: Washington (P), in a federal habeas proceeding, contended that, in a capital sentence hearing, he had been denied effective assistance of counsel.

CONCISE RULE OF LAW: At a capital sentence hearing, a Sixth Amendment violation occurs only if counsel's performance was deficient and such deficiency resulted in actual prejudice.

FACTS: Washington (P) went on a crime spree that resulted in three deaths. He was charged with numerous offenses, including burglary, kidnapping, and murder. Against his attorney's wishes, he confessed. Also against his attorney's advice, he waived a jury. Finally, he pleaded guilty on all counts, again against his attorney's advice. At the sentence hearing, his attorney stressed Washington's (P) absence of a prior criminal record, his generally good character, and alleged mental disturbance due to poor economic circumstances. He did not introduce character witnesses. He neither introduced psychiatric testimony, as he had not been able to find a mental health professional who would testify that Washington (P) was mentally disturbed. The judge, citing numerous aggravating circumstances due to the gruesome nature of the murders, imposed the death sentence. The Florida Supreme Court affirmed. Washington (P) petitioned for a writ of habeas corpus. The district court denied relief, but the Eleventh Circuit reversed. The Supreme Court granted review.

ISSUE: At a capital sentence hearing, will a Sixth Amendment violation occur only if counsel's performance was deficient and such deficiency resulted in actual prejudice?

HOLDING AND DECISION: (O'Connor, J.) Yes. At a capital sentence hearing, a Sixth Amendment violation occurs only if counsel's performance was deficient and such deficiency resulted in actual prejudice. The Sixth Amendment's right to counsel envisions effective assistance of counsel; ineffective assistance is tantamount to no assistance. The purpose of assistance of counsel is to ensure a fair trial. Consequently, ineffectiveness of counsel is that type of ineffectiveness that renders a trial unfair. The proper standard for evaluating effectiveness is that counsel will be considered ineffective if counsel's performance is so deficient that counsel was not functioning as counsel. Further, such deficiency must result in prejudice, as an absence of prejudice removes concerns of trial fairness. Exactly what constitutes a deficient performance by counsel cannot be set out in specific guidelines; rather, counsel's performance must be viewed against professional standards, taking into account the facts reasonably available to counsel at the time of his tactical decisions. It must be emphasized that counsel's competence is to be presumed, and counsel's performance should not be second-guessed with the benefit of hindsight not available to counsel at the time of his decisions. With respect to prejudice, prejudice will not be presumed in other than a narrow set of circumstances, such as corruption or conflict of interest. Applying the foregoing standards to the present case, it is clear that Washington's (P) counsel's performance was far from ineffective. Operating under severe disadvantages, not the least being Washington's (P) habitual rejection of his advice, counsel made certain tactical decisions with respect to evidence and argument that were quite reasonable. Beyond this, the circumstances were so aggravating that it is unlikely that prejudice could have resulted from ineffectiveness even had it occurred. Therefore, no Sixth Amendment violation occurred in this case. Reversed.

DISSENT: (Marshall, J.) The majority opinion is excessively deferential to counsel in several respects. The standard for competency is too lenient and the level of prejudice that needs to be shown for a Sixth Amendment violation to occur excessive. Finally, the Court errs in applying the same standard to capital cases as less crucial cases.

EDITOR'S ANALYSIS: Prior to the present opinion, lower courts had grappled with the same issue, reaching widely varied results. Both objective and subjective standards of competence had been applied. With respect to prejudice, some courts had employed the "outcome-determinative" test the Court used. Others had held prejudice to be presumed.

[For more information on adequate representation, see Casenote Law Outline on Criminal Procedure, Chapter 17, § IV, Right to Effective Representation of Counsel.]

NOTES:

UNITED STATES v. DeCOSTER
624 F.2d 196 (D.C. Cir. 1976).

NATURE OF CASE: Appeal from criminal conviction.

FACT SUMMARY: [The facts were culled from the dissent, the only portion reproduced in the casebook.] DeCoster (D) contended that he was convicted due to ineffective counsel.

CONCISE RULE OF LAW: None stated in casebook excerpt.

FACTS: DeCoster (D), charged with a crime [not stated in the casebook excerpt], contended that counsel had ben ineffective because his counsel had not contacted potential witnesses and had not learned that DeCoster (D) contended that he had acted in self-defense.

ISSUE: None stated in casebook excerpt.

HOLDING AND DECISION: [No portion of the majority opinion was reproduced in the casebook. Chief Judge Bazelon dissented from the majority's view that since no prejudice occurred, counsel's conduct was not determinative.]

DISSENT: (Bazelon, C.J.) The approach for defining ineffective assistance of counsel should focus on counsel's conduct, rather than looking to the effect of such conduct. Clearly, counsel must undertake such matters as conferring with the client as often as necessary, undertaking a reasonable investigation, and disclosing tactical decisions.

EDITOR'S ANALYSIS: The majority's approach here was later validated by the Supreme Court in Strickland v. Washington, 466 U.S. 668 (1984). The Court imposed, as did the District of Columbia Circuit here, a prejudice requirement. Judge Bazelon's dissent was echoed by Justice Marshall, who took essentially the same position.

NOTES:

NIX v. WHITESIDE
475 U.S. 157 (1986).

NATURE OF CASE: Appeal from a reversal of denial of habeas corpus following conviction for murder.

FACT SUMMARY: Whiteside (D), who was dissuaded by his attorney from committing perjury, sought habeas corpus relief for ineffective assistance of counsel.

CONCISE RULE OF LAW: A defendant is not denied effective assistance of counsel if his attorney dissuades him from committing perjury.

FACTS: Whiteside (D) stabbed and killed Love. Prior to the trial, Whiteside (D) told his attorney that he was going to testify that he saw Love holding a gun, something he had earlier stated was not the case. Whiteside's (D) attorney said that he would inform the court of Whiteside's (D) perjury if Whiteside (D) did this, so Whiteside (D) did not make the assertion. Whiteside (D) was convicted, and the conviction was affirmed. A district court denied habeas corpus, but the Eighth Circuit reversed, holding that Whiteside (D) had been denied effective assistance of counsel.

ISSUE: Is a defendant denied effective assistance of counsel if his attorney dissuades him from committing perjury?

HOLDING AND DECISION: (Burger, C.J.) No. A defendant is not denied effective assistance of counsel if his attorney dissuades him from committing perjury. A defendant is denied effective counsel only if counsel's errors are so serious as to amount to not functioning as counsel. An attorney is under an ethical duty to prevent perjury, and counsel's efforts to dissuade were perfectly in keeping with this duty. A defendant does not have a right to testify falsely, and that is the only "right" that Whiteside (D) could possibly have been denied. Therefore, Whiteside's (D) counsel's acts were perfectly proper. Reversed.

CONCURRENCE: (Brennan, J.) The Court has no authority to establish rules of ethical conduct for lawyers practicing in state courts.

CONCURRENCE: (Blackmun, J.) To the extent that Whiteside's (P) claim rests on the assertion that he would have been acquitted had he been able to testify falsely, Whiteside (P) claims a right the law does not recognize and, therefore, has suffered no prejudice.

EDITOR'S ANALYSIS: The duty of an attorney not to tolerate perjury from his client is time-honored. Written guidelines go as far back as 1908, but the tradition goes much further than that. This principle is embodied today in DR 7-102 of the Model Code of Professional Responsibility.

NOTES:

CUYLER v. SULLIVAN
446 U.S. 335 (1980).

NATURE OF CASE: Review of order granting federal habeas corpus.

FACT SUMMARY: Sullivan (P) contended that the trial court erred in not undertaking its own inquiry as to whether his attorney's multiple representation created a possibility of conflict.

CONCISE RULES OF LAW: (1) A state trial judge is under no duty to inquire into the propriety of multiple representation, absent objection. (2) The mere possibility of a conflict of interest does not create a Sixth Amendment violation.

FACTS: Sullivan (P) was indicted with two others for first-degree murder. Two private attorneys represented all three defendants, each tried separately. At no time during this trial did Sullivan (P) object that his counsel had a conflict of interest. After the trial, which resulted in a conviction, Sullivan (P) appealed, both directly and in a state collateral proceeding. The Pennsylvania Supreme Court upheld the conviction. Sullivan (P) then filed a federal habeas action. The district court denied the petition. The Third Circuit reversed, holding that the trial court should have inquired as to the possibility of a conflict. The Supreme Court granted review.

ISSUES: (1) Is a state trial judge under a duty to inquire into the propriety of multiple representation? (2) Does the possibility of a conflict of interest create a Sixth Amendment violation?

HOLDING AND DECISION: (Powell, J.) No. (1) A state trial judge is under no duty to inquire into the propriety of multiple representation, absent objection. (2) No. The mere possibility of a conflict of interest does not create a Sixth Amendment violation. Defense counsel have an ethical obligation to advise the court of conflicts, and such counsel is usually in a better position than the courts to see the conflict arise. Courts rely on counsel in this area, and nothing in this Court's precedent mandates anything to the contrary. With respect to whether the possibility of conflict gives rise to a Sixth Amendment violation, it must be remembered that a Sixth Amendment violation occurs only when counsel is actually ineffective. The possibility of conflict, which exists in almost all cases of multiple representation, is not sufficient to give rise to a violation. Here, the trial court was never informed of any conflict or the potential therefor. No Sixth Amendment violation occurred. Reversed.

CONCURRENCE: (Brennan, J.) When it is clear, as here, that a defendant agreed to joint representation, it is fair to require an actual conflict for a Sixth Amendment violation to be shown.

DISSENT IN PART: (Marshall, J.) The potential for conflict in multiple representation is so grave that a court should make its own inquiry as to possible conflicts.

EDITOR'S ANALYSIS: The level of the Court's analysis was that of the Constitution. It should be remembered that constitutional law only provides a minimum level of rights; statutes can go beyond this level. In the context of this case, Fed. R. Crim. P. 44(c) provides for judicial inquiry as to conflicts in some limited instances.

NOTES:

FARETTA v. CALIFORNIA
422 U.S. 806 (1975).

NATURE OF CASE: Appeal of a conviction for grand theft.

FACT SUMMARY: Faretta (D) was charged with grand theft. Before and during trial, he moved to represent himself. The trial judge refused, and he was convicted.

CONCISE RULE OF LAW: A state may not constitutionally impose a lawyer on a defendant who wishes to represent himself, so long as the defendant has made a knowing and intelligent waiver of his right to a lawyer.

FACTS: Faretta (D) was charged with grand theft. Several weeks before the date of his trial, Faretta (D) requested that he be permitted to defend himself. The trial judge, in a preliminary ruling, accepted Faretta's (D) waiver of counsel. Several weeks later, but still before trial, the judge held a sua sponte hearing to determine Faretta's (D) ability to conduct his own defense, and decided on the basis of Faretta's (D) answers to questions on state law that Faretta (D) had not made a knowing and intelligent waiver of his right to assistance of counsel. The trial judge ruled that Faretta (D) had no constitutional right to conduct his own defense and appointed a public defender to represent him. Faretta (D) was convicted and sentenced to prison. This decision was affirmed by the court of appeals, and the state supreme court refused to hear the case. The U.S. Supreme Court granted certiorari.

ISSUE: Can a state constitutionally impose a lawyer on a defendant who wishes to represent himself, if the defendant has made a knowing and intelligent waiver of his right to a lawyer?

HOLDING AND DECISION: (Stewart, J.) No. A state may not constitutionally impose a lawyer on a defendant who wishes to represent himself so long as the defendant has made a knowing and intelligent waiver of his right to a lawyer. The rationale for this rule lies within the structure of the Sixth Amendment in that it is consistent with the Sixth Amendment's right to make a personal defense. Here, Faretta (D) was literate and competent, and knowingly exercised his free will to make a choice to represent himself. His level of legal knowledge was not relevant to an assessment of his knowing exercise of the right to defend himself. Vacated and remanded.

DISSENT: (Burger, C.J.) Society has an interest in ensuring that trials are fair, and permitting an ill-advised defendant to represent himself undercuts that interest. Moreover, the "right" recognized here is found nowhere in the Constitution.

DISSENT: (Blackmun, J.) No textual support exists in the Constitution for the right created today, and the historical precedent quoted by the Court is suspect. Finally, the rule announced here creates a great capacity for procedural confusion.

EDITOR'S ANALYSIS: The right of an accused to proceed pro se is a constitutional right. Moreover, on the federal level, it is a statutory right as well. However, this right is qualified by the requirement that a waiver of counsel is, taking into account all of the circumstances, knowingly and intelligently made. The trial judge should himself ask the accused about the circumstances of the waiver. If a defendant has successfully waived his right to counsel, a written memorial of this should be made. (Wright, Fed. Prac. & Proc., Vol. 3, at 213-216.)

NOTES:

McKASKLE v. WIGGINS
465 U.S. 168 (1984).

NATURE OF CASE: Review of grant of federal writ of habeas corpus.

FACT SUMMARY: Wiggins (P), a pro se defendant, contended that court-appointed standby counsel's failure to remain silent constituted a Sixth Amendment violation.

CONCISE RULE OF LAW: Standby counsel to a pro se criminal defendant does not commit a Sixth Amendment violation by failing to remain silent.

FACTS: Wiggins (P) was charged with burglary. Prior to trial, he insisted in representing himself. Over his objection, the trial court appointed a public defender as standby counsel. During the course of the trial, Wiggins' (P) attitude toward standby counsel fluctuated: he at first wished to proceed entirely without assistance but later requested that standby counsel conduct voir dire. He later again objected to counsel's presence but then had counsel make closing argument. During the course of the trial, counsel, out of the jury's presence, disagreed with some of Wiggins' (P) tactical decisions. However, Wiggins (P) always had the final say. Wiggins (P) was convicted and sentenced to life imprisonment as a recidivist. This was affirmed on appeal. Wiggins (P) petitioned for a federal writ of habeas corpus. The Fifth Circuit granted the writ, ruling that counsel had overstepped his bounds by not always being silent when so instructed by Wiggins (P). The Supreme Court granted review.

ISSUE: Does standby counsel to a pro se criminal defendant commit a Sixth Amendment violation by failing to remain silent?

HOLDING AND DECISION: (O'Connor, J.) No. Standby counsel to a pro se criminal defendant does not commit a Sixth Amendment violation by failing to remain silent. A criminal defendant has an absolute right to present his own defense. However, respect for these rights does not require that standby counsel, if any, be "seen and not heard." The question is whether the defendant had a fair chance to present his case his own way. He must have control over how the case is presented, and standby counsel cannot be allowed to destroy the jury's perception that the defendant is presenting his own defense. As long as standby counsel does not interfere with these conditions, the defendant has no cause to complain. Here, standby counsel's disagreements with Wiggins (P) were out of the jury's presence, and all the decisions regarding tactics were his. Moreover, his conduct was inconsistent, to say the least, which further mitigates any claim to a Sixth Amendment violation he might have reversed.

EDITOR'S ANALYSIS: This case was a corollary to Faretta v. California, 422 U.S. 806 (1975). That case established the right of a criminal defendant to represent himself. The present decision was the first Supreme Court decision defining how far that right extends.

[For more information on self-representation, see Casenote Law Outline on Criminal Procedure, Chapter 17, § II, Right to Self-Representation at Trial.]

NOTES:

CAPLIN & DRYSDALE, CHARTERED v. UNITED STATES
109 S. Ct. 2646 (1989).

NATURE OF CASE: Review of order refusing to release funds sequestered pursuant to statute.

FACT SUMMARY: Caplin & Drysdale (P) contended that a federal law allowing forfeiture of moneys obtained through drug trafficking was unconstitutional so far as the funds would be used to pay defense costs.

CONCISE RULE OF LAW: A forfeiture statute is not unconstitutional because it prevents a defendant from obtaining private counsel.

FACTS: Reckmeyer (D) was indicted for violations of federal drug trafficking laws. Pursuant to 21 U.S.C. § 853, the Government (P) obtained an order freezing all of Reckmeyer's (D) assets to the extent they were obtained through such trafficking. Reckmeyer (D) eventually pleaded guilty, and the assets were forfeited. Caplin & Drysdale (P), the law firm that had represented Reckmeyer (D), filed a claim against the funds. This was denied by the trial court. The Fourth Circuit held en banc that the forfeiture of funds to be used to pay for counsel violated the Sixth Amendment. The Supreme Court granted review.

ISSUE: Is a forfeiture statute unconstitutional because it prevents a defendant from obtaining private counsel?

HOLDING AND DECISION: (White, J.) No. A forfeiture statute is not unconstitutional because it prevents a defendant from obtaining private counsel. The Sixth Amendment gives an accused the right to effective assistance of counsel; it gives no right to counsel of choice if such counsel is beyond the defendant's means. A defendant has no Sixth Amendment right to spend money that is not lawfully his own on defense. Caplin & Drysdale (P) argued that the interests of the defendant and the government should be "balanced" to decide who has the greater interest in the funds. This is not so because a defendant has no interest in his ill-gotten gains. Even under such an analysis, governmental interest is high. The forfeiture law provides funds to pay for law enforcement and serves to break the power of organized crime. For these reasons, the Fourth Circuit was in error. Reversed.

DISSENT: (Blackmun, J.) The statute represents a grave danger to the administration of justice. It constitutes a powerful tool for the government to decimate the effectiveness of the criminal defense bar and completely upsets the balance of power between the government and criminal defendants. This is completely antithetical to the Sixth Amendment.

EDITOR'S ANALYSIS: Under 21 U.S.C. § 853(n), a party with an interest in sequestered property is permitted to file a claim against it. To qualify under this section, a claimant has to have entered into a bona fide transaction with a defendant and with no reason to believe that the funds were tainted. An attorney representing a defendant would be very unlikely to meet the latter part of the test.

NOTES:

NOTES

CHAPTER 5
THE SIXTH AMENDMENT AND DUE PROCESS APPLIED - THE PROBLEM OF EYEWITNESS IDENTIFICATION

QUICK REFERENCE RULES OF LAW

1. **The Right to Counsel at Lineups.** An accused has the right to counsel at a pretrial lineup. (United States v. Wade)

2. **Lineups before Initiation of Adversary Proceedings.** There is no right to counsel at police lineups held before the accused is arrested or charged with a crime. (Kirby v. Illinois)

    [For more information on lineups before initiation of adversary proceedings, see Casenote Law Outline on Criminal Procedure, Chapter 21, § I, Corporeal Identification Procedures: Right to Counsel.]

3. **Photographic Identification.** A defendant's counsel need not be present at a postindictment photographic display. (United States v. Ash)

    [For more information on photographic identification, see Casenote Law Outline on Criminal Procedure, Chapter 21, § II, Non-corporeal Identification Procedures: Right to Counsel.]

4. **Due Process During Identification Procedures.** If an identification is independently reliable, it will not be excluded solely because police identification techniques were suggestive. (Manson v. Braithwaite)

    [For more information on due process during identification procedures, see Casenote Law Outline on Criminal Procedure, Chapter 21, § III, Identification Procedures: Due Process of Law.]

NOTES

UNITED STATES v. WADE
388 U.S. 218 (1967).

NATURE OF CASE: Review of order reversing conviction of conspiracy and bank robbery.

FACT SUMMARY: Wade (D), accused of bank robbery, was force to undergo a pretrial lineup without benefit of counsel.

CONCISE RULE OF LAW: An accused has the right to counsel at a pretrial lineup.

FACTS: A partially masked gunman robbed a bank and sped away with an accomplice. Wade (D) was later arrested and charged with the crime. At one point, without informing his attorney, authorities displayed him to two witnesses in a lineup format. Both witnesses identified him both at the lineup and later at trial. Wade (D) was convicted of conspiracy and bank robbery. He appealed, contending that absence of counsel had made the identification unconstitutional. The Fifth Circuit agreed and reversed. The Supreme Court granted review.

ISSUE: Does an accused have the right to counsel at a pretrial lineup?

HOLDING AND DECISION: (Brennan, J.) Yes. An accused has the right to counsel at a pretrial lineup. This Court has long held that an accused enjoys the right to counsel not only at trial but at all critical stages of a prosecution where absence of counsel creates an undue risk of an unfair trial. There can be no doubt that a pretrial lineup is such a proceeding. The vagaries of eyewitness identification have probably been the cause of more false convictions than all other reasons combined. A pretrial lineup, which often serves to solidify a witness' memory regarding a suspect, carries great potential for abuse: it can be made unduly suggestive in all manner of ways. A layman cannot be expected to sort through these situations, and, therefore, counsel is a necessary aspect of such proceedings. [The Court went on to disagree with the Fifth Circuit's per se invalidation of the without-counsel lineup and established a standard that if the prosecution could show that the in-court identification occurred independent of the unconstitutional lineup, a conviction could stand. The matter was remanded for such a determination.]

DISSENT: (Black, J.) As long as an unconstitutional lineup identification is not introduced into evidence, no constitutional violation occurs.

DISSENT IN PART: (White, J.) Improperly suggestive police procedures are not so pervasive that a broad prophylactic rule such as that mandated by the Court is necessary. The rule created here infringes on the state interest of prompt identification by witnesses.

EDITOR'S ANALYSIS: There are numerous identification procedures where the right to counsel does not attach. Examples include fingerprinting and body tissue analyses. Unlike lineups, these are relatively quantifiable situations which can be attacked through cross-examination without counsel have been present during the analyses.

NOTES:

KIRBY v. ILLINOIS
406 U.S. 682 (1972).

NATURE OF CASE: Appeal from conviction for robbery.

FACT SUMMARY: Shard was robbed and went to police headquarters. Later, two men were brought into headquarters and Shard identified them as the robbers prior to the robbers being charged or having the right to counsel.

CONCISE RULE OF LAW: There is no right to counsel at police lineups held before the accused is arrested or charged with a crime.

FACTS: Shard reported to the police that two men had robbed him on the street and had taken his wallet containing travelers checks and a Social Security card. The next day, the police stopped Kirby (D) and Bean (D) while investigating an unrelated crime. Kirby (D) produced a wallet that contained three travelers checks and a Social Security card, all bearing the name of Shard. The officer brought the two men to headquarters, but only after arriving and checking the records did the officer learn of the Shard robbery. Shard was picked up and brought to the station by the police. Immediately upon entering the room where Kirby (D) and Bean (D) were seated, Shard positively identified them as his robbers. No lawyer was present and neither suspect had asked for or been advised of any right to the presence of counsel. At the trial, Shard described his identification of the two suspects at the station and identified them again in the courtroom.

ISSUE: Should the Wade-Gilbert exclusionary rule of pretrial identifications at lineups without presence of counsel be extended to identification testimony based upon a confrontation that took place prior to the accused being indicted or otherwise formally charged with a criminal offense?

HOLDING AND DECISION: (Stewart, J.) No. The Wade-Gilbert line of cases stand for the proposition that the accused's right to counsel attaches only after adversary judicial proceedings have been instituted and, therefore, there is no right to counsel at a confrontation held prior to the accused being formally charged. It is only after formal charges have been instituted and the state has decided to prosecute, and only then, that the adverse positions of government and the accused have solidified. It is only then that the accused is faced with prosecution and the intricacies of the law. The Wade-Gilbert rule is that the accused is entitled to counsel at any critical stage of the criminal proceeding, and a post-indictment lineup is a critical stage. This court will not depart from the rationale in those cases. If an accused wishes to attack a pre-indictment confrontation, he must use the Due Process Clause. If the lineup is unnecessarily suggestive and conducive to irreparable mistaken identification, then it can be voided. The rule in Stovall states that one must balance the accused's right to be protected from prejudicial procedures against the interests of society in the prompt and purposeful investigation of crime. The judgment is affirmed.

DISSENT: (Brennan, J.) The initiation of adversary judicial criminal proceedings is completely irrelevant to whether counsel is necessary at a pretrial confrontation for identification.

EDITOR'S ANALYSIS: Kirby reflects a new majority which crystallized in the Burger Court. Kirby can be used to undermine the force and scope of Wade and Gilbert. All the police need do is not formally charge a suspect after they arrest him until they have an opportunity to conduct a lineup. Counsel would not be required in those circumstances.

[For more information on lineups before initiation of adversary proceedings, see Casenote Law Outline on Criminal Procedure, Chapter 21, § I, Corporeal Identification Procedures: Right to Counsel.]

NOTES:

UNITED STATES v. ASH
413 U.S. 300 (1973).

NATURE OF CASE: Appeal from conviction of bank robbery.

FACT SUMMARY: Ash (D) was convicted of bank robbery after witnesses selected his photo from a series of "mug shots," a procedure done outside the presence of his counsel.

CONCISE RULE OF LAW: A defendant's counsel need not be present at a postindictment photographic display.

FACTS: Acting on a tip from an informant, police showed a series of "mug shots" to witnesses to a bank robbery. They all picked Ash's (D) photo. He was indicted for the robbery. Just prior to the trial, the prosecutor repeated the procedure. Ash's (D) counsel was not present. Three of the four witnesses selected Ash's (D) photograph. These witnesses identified Ash (D) in court. He was convicted. The District of Columbia Circuit, sitting en banc, reversed, holding that the Sixth Amendment required that Ash's (D) counsel had to have been present. The Supreme Court granted review.

ISSUE: Must a defendant's counsel be present at a postindictment photographic display?

HOLDING AND DECISION: (Blackmun, J.) No. A defendant's counsel need not be present at a postindictment photographic display. This Court has held that the Sixth Amendment's guarantee of assistance of counsel at trial goes beyond trial itself to critical stages of a prosecution. An analysis of the Court's cases demonstrates that the unifying element in stages that have been identified as being critical is the potential for the prosecution to take undue advantage of a defendant's ignorance of the legal process if counsel is not present. A postindictment photographic display is not such a situation. First, the defendant himself is not present at such a proceeding. Second, the photographs are equally available to the defense for whatever use may be appropriate. Finally, witnesses who identify a defendant in court based on photographic identification are amenable to cross-examination about the suggestiveness of the proceedings. Thus, the court of appeals' holding was erroneous. Reversed.

CONCURRENCE: (Stewart, J.) A pretrial photographic display is more akin to a simple interview than to a pretrial lineup.

DISSENT: (Brennan, J.) As a corporeal identification is usually more accurate than a photographic one, the dangers of misidentification are actually greater at the latter proceeding. Also, the possibilities for impermissible suggestion at a photographic display are no less real than at a lineup. Finally, to the extent that the Court imposes a requirement that to be considered "critical" a defendant must be present at a stage of a prosecution, the Court departs from sound analysis.

EDITOR'S ANALYSIS: In 1967, the Court decided United States v. Wade, 388 U.S. 218. In that case, the Court held that an accused enjoyed the right to counsel at a pretrial lineup. Due to the obvious similarity between a lineup and a photographic display, the Court took some pains in the present opinion to distinguish Wade.

[For more information on photographic identification, see Casenote Law Outline on Criminal Procedure, Chapter 21, § II, Non-corporeal Identification Procedures: Right to Counsel.]

NOTES:

MANSON v. BRATHWAITE
432 U.S. 98 (1977).

NATURE OF CASE: Appeal from the reversal of a conviction for the sale of narcotics.

FACT SUMMARY: Glover, a police officer, after describing the man who had sold him heroin, was given a photograph of the suspect for identification purposes.

CONCISE RULE OF LAW: If an identification is independently reliable, it will not be excluded solely because police identification techniques were suggestive.

FACTS: Glover, an undercover policeman, purchased heroin from Brathwaite (D). During the purchase, which took several minutes, Glover was no more than two or three feet from him. Glover returned to headquarters and described the individual whom he had seen in great detail. From the description another officer pulled a picture of Brathwaite (D) from their files. Glover saw the photograph two days later and promptly identified Brathwaite (D) as the seller. The photograph and identification were subsequently admitted at trial without objection. Brathwaite (D) was found guilty and was sentenced to prison. Fourteen months later, Brathwaite (D) challenged the photographic identification on the grounds that it was too suggestive thereby rendering the identification itself per se excludable. The court of appeals reversed the conviction on this basis holding that independent indicia of reliability could not overcome the suggestibility of the identification technique.

ISSUE: Will independent indicia of reliability allow admissibility of a witness whose original police identification was based on suggestive identification techniques?

HOLDING AND DECISION: (Blackmun, J.) Yes. The circuits have split over whether or not a per se rule should apply to excluding identification based on suggestive identification procedures. Some favor per se exclusion. Others take each case separately in order to determine if the identification would be otherwise reliable, and if so allowing it in evidence. We think the latter theory is correct. To hold otherwise would exclude relevant information from the jury merely because of improper police procedure. The case-by-case approach will be a deterrent to the police and will prevent the guilty from being freed. The linchpin in this area is the independent reliability of the identification. Here, we have a trained police officer who viewed Brathwaite (D) closely for two to three minutes from a short distance. Glover then described Brathwaite (D) in detail shortly thereafter. The pictorial identification was two days later. All of this indicates independent reliability based on a trained observer, a prompt identification, and a reasonable opportunity to view the suspect. Independently reliable identifications need not be excluded to satisfy due process requirements.

CONCURRENCE: (Stevens, J.) While this case is extremely close, I am convinced of the independent reliability of the identification and feel that judicial fiat in constructing per se exclusions is unwarranted.

DISSENT: (Marshall, J.) The Court's "totality of the circumstances" rule ignores both precedent and reason. It will allow seriously unreliable and misleading evidence to be put before juries. Equally important, it will result in erroneous convictions, allowing dangerous criminals to remain on the streets while citizens assume that police action has given them protection. Only a per se rule against admissibility of suggestive lineups can ameliorate these problems.

EDITOR'S ANALYSIS: The per se rule is used to discourage police abuses. The majority appears to indicate that non-police witnesses will be less likely to survive an ad hoc, case-by-case approach because they are more prone to misidentification since they are not trained observers. The stress on them is also deemed greater which may cause faulty identifications. No hard and fast rules can be developed in this area, but the court apparently focuses on: (1) the length of time in which the accused was viewed; (2) the nature of the witness; (3) the circumstances; (4) the length of time between the incident and the identification; and (5) the ability to give an initial description of the accused.

[For more information on due process during identification procedures, see Casenote Law Outline on Criminal Procedure, Chapter 21, § III, Identification Procedures: Due Process of Law.]

NOTES:

CHAPTER 6
THE RISE AND FALL OF BOYD v. UNITED STATES

QUICK REFERENCE RULES OF LAW

1. **Search and Seizure.** It is unconstitutional for the government to mandate production of personal papers in a forfeiture proceeding. (Boyd v. United States)

   [For more information on historical meaning of "search and seizure," see Casenote Law Outline on Criminal Procedure, Chapter 2, § I, "Search": The Old Meaning.]

2. **Search and Seizure.** The use of body tissue evidence against an accused does not violate the Fifth Amendment. (Schmerber v. California)

3. **Seizure of Property.** That an object has evidentiary value only does not render its seizure unconstitutional. (Warden, Maryland Penitentiary v. Hayden)

   [For more information on seizure of property, see Casenote Law Outline on Criminal Procedure, Chapter 2, § IX, "Seizure": Of Property.]

4. **The Fifth Amendment Privilege and Business Records.** Compelled production of business records may violate the Fifth Amendment. (United States v. Doe)

5. **The Fifth Amendment Privilege and Business Records.** A custodian of corporate records may not avoid production thereof on Fifth Amendment grounds. (Braswell v. United States)

NOTES

BOYD v. UNITED STATES
116 U.S. 616 (1886).

NATURE OF CASE: Review of order compelling forfeiture of property.

FACT SUMMARY: Boyd (D) contended that the federal law mandating production of personal papers in a forfeiture proceeding was unconstitutional.

CONCISE RULE OF LAW: It is unconstitutional for the government to mandate production of personal papers in a forfeiture proceeding.

FACTS: The Government (P) instituted a forfeiture proceeding against certain cases of glass belonging to Boyd (D), contending that appropriate customs duties had not been paid. Prior to trial, the Government (P) demanded, pursuant to statute, that Boyd (D) produce certain documentation in his possession. Boyd (D) complied, under objection that it was unconstitutional for the court to compel him to produce personal papers. The trial court ordered the glass forfeited. The Supreme Court granted review.

ISSUE: Is it unconstitutional for the government to mandate production of personal papers in a forfeiture proceeding?

HOLDING AND DECISION: (Bradley, J.) Yes. It is unconstitutional for the government to mandate production of personal papers in a forfeiture proceeding. The Fourth Amendment's guarantee against unreasonable searches and seizures and the Fifth Amendment's protection against self-incrimination technically apply to criminal proceedings. However, a forfeiture proceeding is sufficiently quasi-criminal that the Amendments apply. The law in question, which compels production of personal papers and records, is functionally similar to the odious general warrants and writs of assistance, against which the Fourth and Fifth Amendments were a reaction. To compel production is the equivalent of a search; the contents of such documents may constitute self-incrimination. Consequently, the forced production of personal documents in a forfeiture proceeding constitutes a violation of the Fourth and Fifth Amendments. Reversed.

CONCURRENCE: (Miller, J.) The law at question does compel self-incrimination, but production itself does not constitute search and seizure.

EDITOR'S ANALYSIS: This case is useful as a history lesson in Fourth and Fifth Amendment law but is no longer vital, its major elements all having been abandoned. A forfeiture proceeding without the prospect of a jail sentence would today be seen purely as civil. Also, production of papers is seen neither as a search and seizure nor as self-incrimination.

NOTES:

[For more information on historical meaning of "search and seizure," see Casenote Law Outline on Criminal Procedure, Chapter 2, § I, "Search": The Old Meaning.]

SCHMERBER v. CALIFORNIA
384 U.S. 757 (1966).

NATURE OF CASE: Appeal from conviction of driving under the influence of alcohol.

FACT SUMMARY: Results of blood sample tests on blood taken from Schmerber (D) against his will were used to convict him of drunk driving.

CONCISE RULE OF LAW: The use of body tissue evidence against an accused does not violate the Fifth Amendment.

FACTS: Schmerber (D) was hospitalized after a traffic accident. At the hospital, at the direction of a police officer and over Schmerber's (D) objections, a doctor drew a blood sample. The blood tested at over the legal limit of intoxication for driving. Based on this evidence, Schmerber (D) was convicted of drunk driving. The Supreme Court granted review.

ISSUE: Does the use of body tissue evidence against an accused violated the Fifth Amendment?

HOLDING AND DECISION: (Brennan, J.) No. The use of body tissue evidence against an accused does not violate the Fifth Amendment. The purpose of the Fifth Amendment was to prohibit the practice of the prosecution establishing its case against an accused through the use of the accused's own (and often coerced) testimony. Consequently, an item of evidence falls within the ambit of the Fifth Amendment only if it is testimonial in nature. The privilege does not extend to using nontestimonial aspects of a defendant to incriminate him. Physical evidence regarding an accused, even if it consists of his own tissue, is not testimonial and, therefore, raises no Fifth Amendment implications. [The Court also held that the case did implicate the Fourth Amendment, the seizure of Schmerber's (D) blood having been reasonable under the circumstances.] Reversed.

DISSENT: (Warren, C.J.) The use of body tissue constitutes self-incrimination.

DISSENT: (Black, J.) The use of forcibly extracted tissue has both a testimonial and communicative character to it. Further, neither of these requirements for self-incrimination are to be found in the Fifth Amendment.

DISSENT: (Douglas, J.) This case implicates the Fifth and Fourteenth Amendments' due process–based right to privacy.

DISSENT: (Fortas, J.) The Due Process Clause prohibits the forcible extraction of blood from a suspect.

EDITOR'S ANALYSIS: The Fifth Amendment, on its face, does not limit itself to testimonial self-incrimination. However, it is clear that this was the concern of the drafters of the Amendment. Its framers were concerned with preventing the introduction of Star Chamber–type inquisitorial prosecution systems.

NOTES:

WARDEN, MARYLAND PENITENTIARY v. HAYDEN
387 U.S. 284 (1967).

NATURE OF CASE: Review of order granting federal writ of habeas corpus.

FACT SUMMARY: Seizure of property belonging to Hayden (P), which aided in his conviction, was challenged as unconstitutional because such property had solely evidentiary value.

CONCISE RULE OF LAW: That an object has evidentiary value only does not render its seizure unconstitutional.

FACTS: Authorities conducted a search of Hayden's (P) home and seized certain items of clothing. These items aided in identification and, thus, helped secure a conviction of armed robbery. The conviction was affirmed. Hayden (P) petitioned for a federal writ of habeas corpus. The district court denied the petition, but the Fourth Circuit reversed, holding the items to have had evidentiary value only and, therefore, not to be subject to search and seizure. The Supreme Court granted review.

ISSUE: Does the fact that an object has evidentiary value only render its seizure unconstitutional?

HOLDING AND DECISION: (Brennan, J.) No. That an object has evidentiary value only does not render its seizure unconstitutional. Traditionally, a distinction has been made between, on the one hand, the fruits or instrumentalities of a crime and, on the other, items having value only as evidence of guilt. The traditional rule is that since the government has no interest in such objects apart from securing a conviction, the introduction of such objects constitutes compelled self-incrimination, and, therefore, their original seizure was unreasonable and, consequently, unconstitutional. This is a flawed analysis. First, since such objects are not testimonial in nature, no Fifth Amendment concerns are raised. Secondly, since the Fourth Amendment protects privacy, not property, the traditional rule improperly injects proprietary requirements into Fourth Amendment analysis. Finally, the privacy interests of a citizen in his possessions do not turn on whether they can be characterized as evidence or instrumentality. Therefore, this traditional distinction is improper and is hereby abolished. Reversed.

CONCURRENCE: (Fortas, J.) The ruling here, while correct in this case, improperly dispenses with the "mere evidence" rule in all cases. There are still instances where its application would be proper.

DISSENT: (Douglas, J.) The foundation of the opinion in this case is that evidence such as that at issue here is not testimonial. As this premise is incorrect, the entire opinion founders.

EDITOR'S ANALYSIS: In the case Boyd v. United States, 116 U.S. 616 (1886), the Court held compelled production of documents to violate the Fifth Amendment. Boyd is still technically good law but has been held to, more or less, its own facts. The physical evidence here was clearly not the type of documentary evidence at issue in Boyd.

[For more information on seizure of property, see Casenote Law Outline on Criminal Procedure, Chapter 2, § IX, "Seizure": Of Property.]

NOTES:

UNITED STATES v. DOE
465 U.S. 605 (1984).

NATURE OF CASE: Review of order quashing subpoena.

FACT SUMMARY: Doe (D) contended that compelled production of certain business records violated the Fifth Amendment.

CONCISE RULE OF LAW: Compelled production of business records may violate the Fifth Amendment.

FACTS: Pursuant to a criminal investigation, the Government (P) issued subpoenas for Doe (D) to produce certain financial records. Doe (D) moved to quash the subpoenas, contending that the records were privileged under the Fifth Amendment and that production thereof violated his privilege against self-incrimination. The district court held that act of production to be privileged under the Fifth Amendment. The Third Circuit held the records privileged and affirmed. The Supreme Court granted review.

ISSUE: May compelled production of business records violate the Fifth Amendment?

HOLDING AND DECISION: (Powell, J.) Yes. Compelled production of business records may violate the Fifth Amendment. The Fifth Amendment protects against compelled testimonial self-incrimination. Records voluntarily prepared cannot be said to be the results of compulsion, and, therefore, the records themselves are not privileged. However, to the extent that the act of producing the records is testimonial, in that it has communicative aspects, compelled production may constitute self-incrimination. Here, both courts below held that production in the context of this case did bear testimonial, communicative aspects. This factual issue is best left to lower courts, so this Court will respect such holdings. Since the act of production would be testimonial in this case, Doe's (D) Fifth Amendment privilege was properly upheld. Affirmed in part; reversed in part.

DISSENT: (O'Connor, J.) The Fifth Amendment provides no protection to the contents of private papers.

DISSENT IN PART: (Marshall, J.) This decision should not be read to imply that there can never be Fifth Amendment protection for private papers.

EDITOR'S ANALYSIS: The present case represents another retreat from Boyd v. U.S., 116 U.S. 616 (1886). Boyd had established a Fifth Amendment implication for private papers. The Court has consistently chipped away at Boyd, although it has never been expressly overruled.

NOTES:

BRASWELL v. UNITED STATES
487 U.S. 99 (1988).

NATURE OF CASE: Review of denial of motion to quash subpoena.

FACT SUMMARY: Braswell (P), served with a subpoena duces tecum in his capacity as custodian of corporate records, sought to avoid production on Fifth Amendment grounds.

CONCISE RULE OF LAW: A custodian of corporate records may not avoid production thereof on Fifth Amendment grounds.

FACTS: Braswell (P) was a sole or majority shareholder of several corporations. Federal prosecutors initiated an investigation of the corporations. A grand jury issued a subpoena which was served on Braswell (P) in his capacity as custodian of corporate records. Braswell (P) moved to quash the subpoena, contending that production of the records constituted self-incrimination under the Fifth Amendment. The district court denied the motion, and the Fifth Circuit affirmed. The Supreme Court granted review.

ISSUE: May a custodian of corporate records avoid production thereof on Fifth Amendment grounds?

HOLDING AND DECISION: (Rehnquist, C.J.) No. A custodian of corporate records may not avoid production thereof on Fifth Amendment grounds. The contents of business records are never privileged, but when the act of producing the records has testimonial elements, the Fifth Amendment may be implicated. However, the privilege against self-incrimination is a personal one. When a custodian of corporate records is ordered to produce such records, he is compelled to act in a representative capacity, not in a personal one. The Court has long recognized the "collective entity" rule, which holds that corporate records are not private. This rule applies to the records themselves, as well as to the act of producing them. Consequently, a custodian of records cannot raise a personal Fifth Amendment objection to producing records in his representative capacity. Here, Braswell (P) was called upon to produce corporate records in such a capacity, so he has no Fifth Amendment claim. Affirmed.

DISSENT: (Kennedy, J.) When a custodian of records is personally jeopardized by a compelled production of corporate records, his personal privilege against self-incrimination is most certainly implicated. If such production is to be compelled, the Constitution requires at the very least the grant of immunity for the act of production.

EDITOR'S ANALYSIS: Immunity is the manner in which an investigating or prosecuting authority can proceed over a Fifth Amendment invocation. Essentially, a grant of immunity is a guarantee that information received from the grantee will not be used against him. In most cases, however, if the same information can be obtained from a nonprivileged source, it can be used against the grantee.

NOTES:

NOTES

CASENOTE LEGAL BRIEFS —CRIMINAL PROCEDURE

CHAPTER 7
THE FOURTH AMENDMENT

QUICK REFERENCE RULES OF LAW

1. **Search.** The Fourth Amendment protects a person from search and seizure if, under the circumstances, he has a justifiable expectation of privacy, regardless of whether an actual physical trespass occurred. (Katz v. United States)

    [For more information on search, see Casenote Law Outline on Criminal Procedure, Chapter 2, §§ I-IV.]

2. **Surveillance.** An audiotape made by being placed on the person of a defendant's accomplice/informant is admissible over a Fourth Amendment objection. (United States v. White)

    [For more information on surveillance, see Casenote Law Outline on Criminal Procedure, Chapter 2, § IV, "Search": Surveillance of Conversations.]

3. **Aerial Surveillance.** A warrantless inspection of property from a lawfully flying helicopter does not violate the Fourth Amendment. (Florida v. Riley)

    [For more information on aerial surveillance, see Casenote Law Outline on Criminal Procedure, Chapter 2, § VII, "Search": Aerial Surveillance.]

4. **Seizure of Persons.** A defendant's rights against unlawful arrest will not operate to suppress evidence found prior to physical restraint. (California v. Hodari D.)

    [For more information on the seizure of persons, see Casenote Law Outline on Criminal Procedure, Chapter 2, § X, "Seizure": Of Persons.]

5. **Exclusionary Rule.** The exclusionary rule does not apply to state prosecutions based on seizures by state officials. (Wolf v. Colorado)

6. **Exclusionary Rule.** The exclusionary rule is applicable to searches and seizures by state officials. (Mapp v. Ohio)

    [For more information on the exclusionary rule, see Casenote Law Outline on Criminal Procedure, Chapter 15, § I, General Principles.]

7. **Aguilar Two-Pronged Test.** If an affidavit to obtain a search warrant is based upon an informer's tip (i.e., hearsay), then the affidavit must state why the informer is "reliable" and the "underlying circumstances" from which the informer drew his conclusions, so as to enable an independent magistrate to conclude that the informer's information provides probable cause for the search. (Spinelli v. United States)

    [For more information on the Aguilar two-pronged test, see Casenote Law Outline on Criminal Procedure, Chapter 3, § III, The Aguilar Two-Pronged Test.]

8. **Totality-of-the-Circumstances Test.** If corroborating evidence exists, a warrant may issue on the basis of a tip of questionable reliability. (Illinois v. Gates)

    [For more information on the totality-of-the-circumstances test, see Casenote Law Outline on Criminal Procedure, Chapter 3, § IV, The Gates Totality-of-the-Circumstances Test.]

9. **Search Incident to Arrest.** Materials seized pursuant to a search incident to a lawful arrest are not inadmissible despite the absence of a warrant. (Warden, Maryland Penitentiary v. Hayden)

   [For more information on search incident to arrest, see Casenote Law Outline on Criminal Procedure, Chapter 7, § II, Scope of the Warrant Exception: In General.]

10. **Automobile Searches.** Where there is probable cause to believe that vehicles are carrying contraband or fruits of the crime, warrantless searches of automobiles are permissible, even where the car itself is seized and held without a warrant for whatever period is necessary to obtain a warrant for the search. (Chambers v. Maroney)

    [For more information on automobile searches, see Casenote Law Outline on Criminal Procedure, Chapter 8, Search Warrant Exception: Automobile Searches.]

11. **Warrantless Search of an Automobile.** Police do not need probable cause to search an entire vehicle to search a container found therein. (California v. Acevedo)

    [For more information on the warrantless search of an automobile, see Casenote Law Outline on Criminal Procedure, Chapter 8, § I, General Rules.]

12. **Arrests in the Home.** Police may not enter a person's home to make a routine felony arrest without a warrant. (Payton v. New York)

    [For more information on arrests in the home, see Casenote Law Outline on Criminal Procedure, Chapter 4, § II, Warrants: In-Home Arrests.]

13. **Administrative Searches.** Routine housing and building code inspections require a search warrant. (Camara v. Municipal Court of San Francisco)

    [For more information on administrative searches, see Casenote Law Outline on Criminal Procedure, Chapter 13, § I, Administrative Code Inspections.]

14. **"Stop and Frisk."** Police may stop and frisk an individual whom they reasonably suspect may be armed and dangerous, even if probable cause to arrest is not present. (Terry v. Ohio)

    [For more information on "stop and frisk," see Casenote Law Outline on Criminal Procedure, Chapter 12, § I, Terry v. Ohio: The Case.]

15. **Scope of Search Incident to Arrest.** A search incident to a lawful arrest cannot be of unlimited scope. (Chimel v. California)

    [For more information on scope of search incident to arrest, see Casenote Law Outline on Criminal Procedure, Chapter 7, § II, Scope of the Warrant Exception: In General.]

16. **Scope of Search Incident to Arrest.** Police may conduct a full search of the person following a lawful arrest. (United States v. Robinson)

17. **Automobile Searches Incident to an Arrest.** When police have made a lawful custodial arrest of the occupant of an automobile, they may, as a contemporaneous incident of that arrest, search the passenger compartment of the automobile. (New York v. Belton)

    [For more information on automobile searches incident to an arrest, see Casenote Law Outline on Criminal Procedure, Chapter 7, § III, Special Rule: Search of an Automobile Incident to an Arrest.]

18. **Inventory Inspection.** A police inventory inspection may involve the opening of closed containers. (Colorado v. Bertine)

   [For more information on inventory inspection, see Casenote Law Outline on Criminal Procedure, Chapter 10, § I, Automobile Inventories.]

19. **Searches and Seizures by Roving Patrols.** Authorities may not conduct random checks of drivers' licenses and registrations. (Delaware v. Prouse)

20. **Searches and Seizures by Roving Patrols.** A state may institute random sobriety checkpoints on highways. (Michigan State Police v. Sitz)

21. **The Seizure and Search of Persons Present at Searched Premises.** A person incidentally on premises subject to a search warrant may not be searched absent independent probable cause therefor. (Ybarra v. Illinois)

22. **Auto Searches.** Occupants of a house being searched pursuant to a warrant may be detained during the search. (Michigan v. Summers)

   [For more information on auto searches, see Casenote Law Outline on Criminal Procedure, Chapter 7, § I, General Rules.]

23. **Searches of Autos.** Contraband discovered pursuant to a search for a vehicle identification number may be constitutionally seized. (New York v. Class)

   [For more information on searches of autos, see Casenote Law Outline on Criminal Procedure, Chapter 8, § I, General Rules.]

24. **The Relationship between Reasonableness and Probable Cause.** A warrant may be issued to search a nonsuspect's property for evidence of a crime without the authorities having first attempted to subpoena the evidence. (Zurcher v. Stanford Daily)

25. **Apprehension.** Deadly force may not be used to apprehend a fleeing felony suspect unless there is probable cause to believe that the suspect poses a significant threat to the safety of others. (Tennessee v. Garner)

   [For more information on apprehension, see Casenote Law Outline on Criminal Procedure, Chapter 2, § X, "Seizure": Of Persons.]

26. **Voluntariness of Consent.** To be voluntary, consent to a search need not include a police admonition that consent may be withheld. (Schneckloth v. Bustamonte)

   [For more information on voluntariness of consent, see Casenote Law Outline on Criminal Procedure, Chapter 11, § II, Lawful Consent: The "Voluntariness" Principle.]

27. **Standing.** Passengers in automobiles who have no claimed relation to the automobile or the property seized do not have standing simply because they were legitimately on the premises at the time of the search. (Rakas v. Illinois)

   [For more information on standing, see Casenote Law Outline on Criminal Procedure, Chapter 14, § II, Rakas v. Illinois.]

28. **Standing.** An evaluation of the totality of the circumstances will be made to determine whether an individual had a reasonable expectation of privacy in the place searched by the police. (Rawlings v. Kentucky)

CASENOTE LEGAL BRIEFS —CRIMINAL PROCEDURE

[For more information on standing, see Casenote Law Outline on Criminal Procedure, Chapter 14, § III, Where the Law Is Now.]

29. **The Fruit of the Poisonous Tree.** In cases where an illegal search enables the police to locate a witness, the witness' statements will be less readily excluded as the fruit of illegal police conduct and a more direct link will be required before exclusion is allowed. (United States v. Ceccolini)

    [For more information on the fruit of the poisonous tree, see Casenote Law Outline on Criminal Procedure, Chapter 15, § V, "Fruit of the Poisonous Tree" Doctrine.]

30. **The Fruit of the Poisonous Tree.** A witness' in-court identification of the defendant may not be excluded as being the fruit of an illegal detention of the defendant. (United States v. Crews)

    [For more information on fruit of the poisonous tree, see Casenote Law Outline on Criminal Procedure, Chapter 15, § V, "Fruit of the Poisonous Tree" Doctrine.]

31. **The Good-faith Exception to the Exclusionary Rule.** Evidence will not be excluded where police rely in good faith on a defective search warrant. (United States v. Leon)

    [For more information on the good-faith exception to the exclusionary rule, see Casenote Law Outline on Criminal Procedure, Chapter 5, § IV, "Particularity."]

KATZ v. UNITED STATES
389 U.S. 347 (1967).

NATURE OF CASE: Appeal from criminal conviction for transmitting betting information over the phone.

FACT SUMMARY: Katz (D) was arrested for transmitting wagering information by telephone to another state; at his trial the government introduced recordings of his conversation made by attaching a listening and recording device to the outside of a phone booth.

CONCISE RULE OF LAW: The Fourth Amendment protects a person from search and seizure if, under the circumstances, he has a justifiable expectation of privacy, regardless of whether an actual physical trespass occurred.

FACTS: Katz (D) was arrested and convicted for transmitting betting information by telephone to another state in violation of a federal statute. At his trial, the prosecution introduced recordings of phone conversations Katz (D) had made. These recordings were made by attaching a recording and listening device to the outside of a phone booth that Katz (D) used to make his calls. There was no search warrant. The government used this device only after it had made an investigation which indicated that the phone booth was being used to transmit such information, and they only recorded conversations that Katz (D) personally had.

ISSUE: Is the attachment of a listening device to the outside of a public telephone booth a search and seizure within the meaning of the Fourth Amendment?

HOLDING AND DECISION: (Stewart, J.) Yes. The Fourth Amendment protects a person's justifiable expectations of privacy, and protects people and not places. Whatever a person knowingly exposes to the public, even in his own home, is therefore not protected by the Fourth Amendment, but what a person keeps private, even in a public place, may be protected. Earlier cases stated that a surveillance without a trespass or seizure of a material object is outside of the Fourth Amendment, and now these cases must be overturned. Even though the phone booth was a public place, and there was no physical trespass (the device was on the outside of the booth), there was a search because the government violated the privacy upon which Katz (D) justifiably relied. There also is a seizure even though no tangible property was taken because the recording of a statement overheard, even if there is no trespass, is a seizure. The remaining question, then, is whether the government complied with the constitutional standards of the Fourth Amendment. Although the government reasonably believed that the phone booth was being illegally used, and their search and seizure was carefully limited both in scope and duration, the action cannot be upheld because there was no search warrant issued. A search warrant is a safeguard in several ways: a neutral magistrate on the basis of information presented to him determined whether a warrant should issue; the search warrant carefully limits the scope of the search; and the government must report back on the evidence it finds. Without such safeguards, even if the search was in fact reasonable, it cannot be upheld.

CONCURRENCE: (Douglas, J.) This case does not determine whether a search warrant would be required in a situation involving the national security. But the Fourth Amendment does not distinguish between types of crimes, so in all investigations, even if national security is involved, a search warrant must issue.

CONCURRENCE: (Harlan, J.) The key to this decision is that one has a reasonable expectation of privacy when he shuts the doors of a telephone booth behind him and pays the fee for use of the telephone.

DISSENT: (Black, J.) The words of the Fourth Amendment do not bear the meaning that the Court gives them in this decision, nor is it the role of the Court to rewrite them to bring them into harmony with the times, as it has done.

DISSENT: (Black, J.) When the Fourth Amendment was adopted, eavesdropping was a common practice, and if the framers of the Constitution wished to limit that procedure they would have used appropriate language. This case, then, goes against the plain meaning of the Fourth Amendment which was solely aimed at limiting the practice of breaking into buildings and seizing tangible property. Therefore, wiretapping, which is a form of eavesdropping, is not subject to the Fourth Amendment.

EDITOR'S ANALYSIS: Katz rejects the old rule which held that there was no search unless there was a physical trespass and substitutes a new rule based on the defendant's expectation of privacy. One facet of this privacy concept is the place involved — for example, if, unlike Katz, the defendant had engaged in conversation in a public place that was audible to others, there would be no search within the meaning of the Fourth Amendment. Also, the privacy concept turns on action of the defendant. If he had engaged in a loud conversation even in his own home which was audible to a person standing outside of his door, there would be no search since the conversation was exposed by the defendant to the public.

[For more information on search, see Casenote Law Outline on Criminal Procedure, Chapter 2, §§ I-IV.]

NOTES:

UNITED STATES v. WHITE
401 U.S. 745 (1971).

NATURE OF CASE: Review of reversal of narcotics convictions.

FACT SUMMARY: White (D) was convicted of illegal narcotics transactions following introduction of an audiotape made on the person of a Government (P) informant.

CONCISE RULE OF LAW: An audiotape made by being placed on the person of a defendant's accomplice/informant is admissible over a Fourth Amendment objection.

FACTS: White (D) and accomplice Jackson effected certain illegal narcotics transactions. Unbeknownst to White (D), Jackson was a Government (P) informant who was "wired" with audiotape equipment. White (D) was indicted. At trial, because Jackson could not be located by the Government (P), it introduced, over White's (D) Fourth Amendment objection, incriminating tapes made on Jackson's person. White (D) was convicted, but the Seventh Circuit reversed. The Supreme Court granted review.

ISSUE: Is an audiotape made by being placed on the person of a defendant's accomplice/informant admissible over a Fourth Amendment objection?

HOLDING AND DECISION: (White, J.) Yes. An audiotape made by being placed on the person of a defendant's accomplice/informant is admissible over a Fourth Amendment objection. Whether the Fourth Amendment is implicated by a search depends upon whether the party invoking the amendment had a reasonable expectation of privacy. In the context of this case, one venturing on a criminal enterprise must be presumed to be aware of the occupational hazard of an accomplice being or becoming an informant. This being established, it is of no moment as to how the informant provides incriminating evidence — live testimony or electronic recording. Consequently, White (D) had no reasonable expectation of privacy here. Reversed.

CONCURRENCE: (Black, J.) The Court's "expectation of privacy" test remains flawed.

DISSENT: (Douglas, J.) The Court equates electronic surveillance with eavesdropping, but the former has a far greater capacity to invade one's privacy.

DISSENT: (Harlan, J.) The proper analysis here is to assess the nature of a practice and the likely extent of its impact upon the individual. Here, electronic recording poses a far greater potential to curb individual liberty than standard informing.

EDITOR'S ANALYSIS: The present case was a plurality opinion — only three other justices joined Justice White's opinion. In such cases, one must look to the concurrences to assess the case's precedential value. Here, Justice Black concurred for reasons basically unrelated to the Court's reasoning, thus diminishing the value of this case as sound precedent.

[For more information on surveillance, see Casenote Law Outline on Criminal Procedure, Chapter 2, § IV, "Search": Surveillance of Conversations.]

NOTES:

FLORIDA v. RILEY
488 U.S. 445 (1989).

NATURE OF CASE: Review of grant of motion to suppress in narcotics prosecution.

FACT SUMMARY: Riley (D) contended that a police officer's visual inspection of his property from a helicopter violated the Fourth Amendment.

CONCISE RULE OF LAW: A warrantless inspection of property from a lawfully flying helicopter does not violate the Fourth Amendment.

FACTS: Acting on a tip, a police officer flew a helicopter over Riley's (D) property. The property contained a greenhouse, some top panels of which were missing. The officer was able to observe marijuana growing in the greenhouse. From this observation a warrant issued, and Riley (D) was charged with a narcotics law violation. The trial court granted Riley's (D) suppression motion, agreeing that the inspection had violated the Fourth Amendment. The state court of appeals reversed, but the Florida Supreme Court reinstated the order. The Supreme Court granted review.

ISSUE: Does a warrantless inspection of property from a lawfully flying helicopter violate the Fourth Amendment?

HOLDING AND DECISION: (White, J.) No. A warrantless inspection of property from a lawfully flying helicopter does not violate the Fourth Amendment. What a person knowingly exposes to the public, even in his own home or office, is not subject to Fourth Amendment protection. What the public is free to see, so are the police. Here, it is not unheard of for helicopters to pass over airspace above residences, and it is foreseeable that items left in plain view will be seen. The helicopter operated by the police was flying in a lawful manner, and, therefore, Riley (D) had no right to expect that items in view from such a craft could not be seen. Consequently, no Fourth Amendment violation occurred. Reversed.

CONCURRENCE: (O'Connor, J.) The plurality places too much reliance on lawful aircraft operation. As long as the operation is foreseeable, its lawfulness is not determinative.

DISSENT: (Brennan, J.) The plurality places undue emphasis on the legality of an observation. That a policeman's act is legal does not make a search necessarily constitutional. Here, the point of observation was not so common a vantage point that a person would expect to be observed therefrom.

DISSENT: (Blackmun, J.) Riley's (D) expectation of privacy and not the lawfulness of the flight from where the surveillance occurred should be the starting point for determining the lawfulness of the search.

EDITOR'S ANALYSIS: The result here was largely dictated by the prior case California v. Ciraolo, 476 U.S. 207 (1986). There, a police officer had viewed contraband from a fixed wing aircraft. As in the present case, the search was held not to implicate the Fourth Amendment.

[For more information on aerial surveillance, see Casenote Law Outline on Criminal Procedure, Chapter 2, § VII, "Search": Aerial Surveillance.]

NOTES:

CALIFORNIA v. HODARI D.
111 S. Ct. 1547 (1991).

NATURE OF CASE: Review of order suppressing evidence pursuant to a criminal prosecution.

FACT SUMMARY: Hodari (D) sought to suppress contraband tossed away after a police officer came upon him but prior to his personal restraint.

CONCISE RULE OF LAW: A defendant's rights against unlawful arrest will not operate to suppress evidence found prior to physical restraint.

FACTS: Two police officers came upon several persons, including Hodari (D), acting in a suspicious manner. When they approached, all took flight. Hodari (D) inadvertently ran in the direction of one officer, whom he did not see until he was almost upon the officer. As soon as he saw the officer, he tossed away an object that later proved to be rock cocaine. Charged with possession, Hodari (D) moved to suppress the evidence on the grounds that the evidence was obtained in an unlawful seizure in violation of the Fourth and Fourteenth Amendments. The trial court denied the motion, but the state court of appeal reversed. The U.S. Supreme Court granted certiorari.

ISSUE: Will a defendant's right against unlawful arrest operate to suppress evidence found prior to physical restraint?

HOLDING AND DECISION: (Scalia, J.) No. A defendant's right against unlawful arrest will not operate to suppress evidence found prior to physical restraint. The Fourth Amendment protects against unlawful seizure. "Seizure," when applied to the person, as it must be in the context of arrest, can only refer to physical restraint. The term "seizure," as it is commonly understood, implies some form of custody or control. Consequently, any evidence found prior to such custody or control cannot be said to be the fruit of an illegal seizure. Here, Hodari (D) had not been placed under physical restraint when he attempted to conceal the incriminating evidence, so the evidence should not have been suppressed. Reversed.

DISSENT: (Stevens, J.) The Court has essentially concluded that than unlawful attempt at an arrest does not implicate the Fourth Amendment. This is at odds with precedent and logic.

EDITOR'S ANALYSIS: United States v. Mendenhall, 446 U.S. 544 (1980), had held that a person is seized only if a person's freedom of movement is restrained. Hodari (D) argued that the presence of an officer alone could work to constitute such a restraint. The Court disagreed, noting that Mendenhall did not say an arrest was necessarily effected when movement is restrained, but rather that an arrest cannot occur absent such restraint. The dissent declared this a distinction without a difference.

NOTES:

[For more information on the seizure of persons, see Casenote Law Outline on Criminal Procedure, Chapter 2, § X, "Seizure": Of Persons.]

WOLF v. COLORADO
338 U.S. 25 (1949).

NATURE OF CASE: Review of criminal conviction.

FACT SUMMARY: Wolf (D) contended that the exclusionary rule applied to state prosecutions based on seizures by state officials.

CONCISE RULE OF LAW: The exclusionary rule does not apply to state prosecutions based on seizures by state officials.

FACTS: Wolf (D) was charged with a crime [not specified in the casebook opinion]. He contended that certain evidence seized by state officials should have been excluded in that the search violated the standards of the Fourth Amendment. The trial court rejected the contention, and Wolf (D) was convicted. The Colorado Supreme Court affirmed, and the Supreme Court granted review.

ISSUE: Does the exclusionary rule apply to state prosecutions based on seizures by state officials?

HOLDING AND DECISION: (Frankfurter, J.) No. The exclusionary rule does not apply to state prosecutions based on seizures by state officials. The Due Process Clause of the Fourteenth Amendment does not necessarily incorporate the Bill of Rights; rather, it reflects matters implicit in the concept of ordered liberty. There can be no question but that the principles protected by the Fourth Amendment are an example of such matters, so the Fourteenth Amendment protects them. However, the ways of enforcing them under the Fourteenth Amendment need not be the same as those under the Fourth Amendment. For the most part, states do provide protection against unlawful searches and seizures. Moreover, state officials are presumably more likely to be influenced by local public opinion, making official misdeeds less likely at the state than federal levels. For these reasons, due process does not require imposition of the exclusionary rule at the state level. Affirmed.

DISSENT: (Murphy, J.) Imposition of the exclusionary rule is the only way this Court can protect a citizen against unreasonable searches and seizures, and the Court should provide such protection.

DISSENT: (Rutledge, J.) The opinion should not be read to suggest that Congress can enact exemptions to the exclusionary rule.

EDITOR'S ANALYSIS: As the opinion states, the Due Process Clause does not incorporate the Bill of Rights. Some have argued for this, most notably Justice Black. The argument is by now academic, as the Court has held due process to embody most of the principles found in the Bill of Rights.

NOTES:

MAPP v. OHIO
367 U.S. 643 (1961).

NATURE OF CASE: Review of conviction for possession of obscene materials.

FACT SUMMARY: Mapp (D), having been subjected to a warrantless search of her premises by city police, contended that contraband found therein should be suppressed.

CONCISE RULE OF LAW: The exclusionary rule is applicable to searches and seizures by state officials.

FACTS: Police entered Mapp's (D) premises without a warrant. Inside, they found pornographic photos and literature. She was charged with possession of obscene material. At trial, she contended that the materials seized should have been suppressed. The motion was denied, and she was convicted. The Ohio Supreme Court affirmed. An appeal to the U.S. Supreme Court was taken.

ISSUE: Is the exclusionary rule applicable to searches and seizures by state officials?

HOLDING AND DECISION: (Clark, J.) Yes. The exclusionary rule is applicable to searches and seizures by state officials. This Court has held that the Due Process Clause of the Fourteenth Amendment incorporates the Fourth Amendment. However, the Court declined to extend the exclusionary rule, created to enforce the rule, to state prosecutions. This approach has now been shown to be erroneous. Time has demonstrated that other approaches to combat illegal searches and seizures at the state level have proved fruitless. Also, various procedural problems with enforcing the rule have been corrected through judicial decision. Most importantly, it is necessary that government at all levels be compelled to obey its own laws, as a failure to do so destroys its legitimacy and breeds contempt for law and order. The exclusionary rule has been shown to be the best vehicle to compel such obedience and for that reason should be as applicable to the states as it is to the federal government. Reversed.

CONCURRENCE: (Black, J.) The Fourth Amendment does not in itself justify the exclusionary rule, but when combined with the Fifth Amendment, such justification exists.

CONCURRENCE: (Douglas, J.) The asymmetry in this area of law should properly be ended.

DISSENT: (Harlan, J.) The exclusionary rule is a rule of procedure which should not be imposed by this Court upon the court systems of sovereign states.

EDITOR'S ANALYSIS: With the possible exception of the Miranda rule, no Supreme Court action in criminal procedure has been as criticized as the exclusionary rule. It has been attacked as failing to achieve its deterrence goal despite a high social cost. The opposition to the rule was perhaps best stated by Judge (later Justice) Cardozo, who described it thusly: "letting the criminal go free because the constable erred." Later cases have narrowed the exclusionary rule to limit suppression to knowing violations of search and seizure rules by police where deterrence should have its greatest effect.

[For more information on the exclusionary rule, see Casenote Law Outline on Criminal Procedure, Chapter 15, § I, General Principles.]

NOTES:

SPINELLI v. UNITED STATES
394 U.S. 410 (1969).

NATURE OF CASE: Appeal from conviction of violation of gambling statutes.

FACT SUMMARY: Spinelli (D) was convicted upon evidence seized with a search warrant, which was issued based upon an affidavit containing a statement from an anonymous informer and information from FBI agents.

CONCISE RULE OF LAW: If an affidavit to obtain a search warrant is based upon an informer's tip (i.e., hearsay), then the affidavit must state why the informer is "reliable" and the "underlying circumstances" from which the informer drew his conclusions, so as to enable an independent magistrate to conclude that the informer's information provides probable cause for the search.

FACTS: Spinelli (D) was convicted of violation of gambling statutes based upon evidence seized by the FBI under a search warrant. The FBI obtained this warrant based upon an affidavit containing the following information: (1) the FBI had been informed by a reliable informer that Spinelli (D) was using two specific telephones to conduct gambling operations; (2) that Spinelli (D) had been seen entering the apartment in which these two telephones were located; and (3) that Spinelli (D) had a reputation as a gambler. Upon conviction, and affirmance of that conviction by the court of appeals, Spinelli (D) brought a petition of certiorari to this court challenging the constitutionality of the issuance of the search warrant.

ISSUE: Is an affidavit based primarily upon an informer's tip, which does not state why the informer is reliable or the "underlying circumstances" as to how the informer obtained his information, sufficient to establish probable cause for the issuance of a search warrant?

HOLDING AND DECISION: (Harlan, J.) No. If an affidavit to obtain a search warrant is based upon an informer's tip (i.e., hearsay), then the affidavit must state why the informer is "reliable" and the "underlying circumstances" from which the informer drew his conclusions, so as to enable an independent magistrate to conclude that the informer's information provides probable cause for the search. Of course, in the absence of a statement detailing how the informer's tip was gathered, a search warrant may still issue if (1) the tip describes the accused's criminal activity in such detail (Draper) that a magistrate may conclude that it was gained in a reliable manner, or (2) there is sufficient independent corroboration of criminal activity in the affidavit so that a magistrate may conclude that there is probable cause that a crime is being committed. Here, first, the tip is insufficient for the issuance of a warrant. The affidavit neither states why the informer was considered reliable nor how he obtained his information. Second, there is no sufficient corroboration of the tip. The fact that Spinelli (D) entered an apartment with two telephones contains no suggestion of criminal activity by itself, and the fact that Spinelli (D) is known as a gambler is only "suspicion" entitled to no weight. Judgment below reversed.

DISSENT: (Black, J.) Lower courts are in a better position to assess probable cause than this Court.

DISSENT: (Fortas, J.) This Court in Aguilar recognized that if an informer's tip has been supplemented by facts obtained as the result of surveillance, that tip should be considered reliable. Here, the affidavit showed relevant surveillance, additional specific facts of significance and adequate reliability (i.e., the informer's tip was substantiated on the facts that Spinelli (D) was using certain telephones).

EDITOR'S ANALYSIS: This case illustrates the two-pronged Aguilar test applicable to affidavits for search warrants based upon hearsay. And Harris v. U.S. (1971) further specified a situation in which a search warrant may be issued on the basis of hearsay. In Harris a warrant was upheld based upon hearsay because the affidavit contained sufficient information to allow the magistrate to determine that there was probable cause for a search warrant. The affidavit contained: (1) the informer's "personal and recent observations" of the accused's criminal activity; (2) the informer's statement which was against his own "penal interest"; and (3) the fact that the officer himself had certain knowledge of the accused's background consistent with the illegal activity alleged. Note, finally, that police do not have to reveal the identity of their informer on a hearing on the issue of probable cause, although they must do so when it is material at trial to establish guilt or innocence.

[For more information on the Aguilar two-pronged test, see Casenote Law Outline on Criminal Procedure, Chapter 3, § III, The Aguilar Two-Pronged Test.]

NOTES:

ILLINOIS v. GATES
462 U.S. 213 (1983).

NATURE OF CASE: Review of order granting motion to suppress.

FACT SUMMARY: The trial court suppressed certain contraband found in a search made on Gates' (D) property because the warrant had been procured due to an anonymous tip of questionable reliability.

CONCISE RULE OF LAW: If corroborating evidence exists, a warrant may issue on the basis of a tip of questionable reliability.

FACTS: City police received an anonymous letter that the Gateses (D) were engaged in a narcotics enterprise. The letter was detailed but revealed nothing of the informant's reliability. State and federal agents began conducting surveillance upon the Gateses (D). At one point, Lance Gates (D) went on a brief trip to Florida. Based on the letter and Gates' (D) trip to Florida, a warrant issued. A search of the Gateses' (D) car and home revealed narcotics and other contraband. At a suppression hearing, the trial court concluded that since the letter was anonymous and gave no indication for reliability of the informant, it was insufficient to provide a basis for a warrant. The contraband was suppressed. The Illinois Supreme Court affirmed, and the Supreme Court granted review.

ISSUE: If corroborating evidence exists, may a warrant issue on the basis of a tip of questionable reliability?

HOLDING AND DECISION: (Rehnquist, J.) Yes. If corroborating evidence exists, a warrant may issue on the basis of a tip of questionable reliability. This Court has established a "two-prong" analysis for warrants to issue on the basis of informant statements, one prong being reliability and the other being knowledge. Many courts, including the court below, have considered this to mean that both requirements must independently be shown. This is an improper analysis. Probable cause is a fluid analysis and is best assessed under a totality-of-the-circumstances approach. If an informant is known to be very reliable, probable cause may exist even if his knowledge is questionable. If the tipper seems very knowledgeable about relevant facts, less reliability needs to be shown. Here, the anonymous letter was quite detailed and was supported by Lance Gates' (D) activities and confirmed by agents' surveillance. This strong showing of knowledgeability rendered the lack of demonstrable reliability nonfatal to the warrant. Reversed.

CONCURRENCE: (White, J.) The corroboration went not only to knowledge but to reliability as well. Reliability remains a condition precedent to probable cause.

DISSENT: (Stevens, J.) The letter and the agents' observations were insufficient to meet the twin tests of reliability and knowledge.

EDITOR'S ANALYSIS: The "two-prong" test arose out of the cases Aguilar v. Texas, 378 U.S. 108 (1964), and Spinelli v. United States, 383 U.S. 410 (1969). These cases reflected a concern that informants constituted an opportunity for abuse of discretion in the issuance of warrants. The two-prong test, repudiated by the Court in the present decision, was the Court's effort to address this perceived problem.

[For more information on the totality-of-the-circumstances test, see Casenote Law Outline on Criminal Procedure, Chapter 3, § IV, The Gates Totality-of-the-Circumstances Test.]

NOTES:

WARDEN, MARYLAND PENITENTIARY v. HAYDEN
387 U.S. 294 (1967).

NATURE OF CASE: Review of order granting habeas corpus.

FACT SUMMARY: Police found incriminating evidence in Hayden's (P) residence when they searched it while effecting his arrest.

CONCISE RULE OF LAW: Materials seized pursuant to a search incident to a lawful arrest are not inadmissible despite the absence of a warrant.

FACTS: After a taxicab was robbed, witnesses followed the robber to Hayden's (P) residence and radioed this fact to police. The police arrived and were given admission by Hayden's (P) wife. They found Hayden (P) upstairs, feigning sleep. When no other men were found in the house, Hayden (P) was arrested. The police searched the house, where they found clothing and a firearm that matched that attributed to the robber by the victim. At trial, these were admitted over Hayden's (P) objection. He was convicted of armed robbery, and this was affirmed on appeal. Hayden (P) filed a federal habeas corpus action, arguing that the evidence was seized without a warrant. The Fourth Circuit granted habeas, and the Supreme Court granted review.

ISSUE: Are materials seized pursuant to a search incident to a lawful arrest inadmissible if a warrant is absent?

HOLDING AND DECISION: (Brennan, J.) No. Materials seized pursuant to a search incident to a lawful arrest are not inadmissible despite the absence of a warrant. When a lawful arrest is made, police may make any search reasonably necessary to effect the arrest. Any items found pursuant to the arrest are not rendered inadmissible due to the lack of a warrant. Here, the police were lawfully in Hayden's (P) residence, and his arrest was lawful. The search of the house was necessary to discover the firearm Hayden (P) was believed to have. Thus, the materials found pursuant to the search were admissible. Reversed.

EDITOR'S ANALYSIS: The search incident to a lawful arrest constitutes one of the major exceptions to the general rule that warrants are required for a search. The exception is largely based on the premise that a search is required to guarantee that no weapons are hidden away. This is particularly relevant if the arrest occurs at the suspect's home.

[For more information on search incident to arrest, see Casenote Law Outline on Criminal Procedure, Chapter 7, § II, Scope of the Warrant Exception: In General.]

NOTES:

CHAMBERS v. MARONEY
399 U.S. 42 (1970).

NATURE OF CASE: Appeal from a robbery conviction.

FACT SUMMARY: Chambers (D) contended that the search of an automobile taken to the station house after his arrest was invalid.

CONCISE RULE OF LAW: Where there is probable cause to believe that vehicles are carrying contraband or fruits of the crime, warrantless searches of automobiles are permissible, even where the car itself is seized and held without a warrant for whatever period is necessary to obtain a warrant for the search.

FACTS: Chambers (D) was indicted for robbing two gas stations. Partially because of a witness' statement that one of the robbers was wearing a green sweater, and that the robbers were driving a station wagon, Chambers (D) was arrested, and the station wagon was taken to the police station and searched. There was no warrant. Search of the station wagon revealed evidence linking Chambers (D) with the crimes. The materials taken from the station wagon were admitted into evidence. Chambers (D) was convicted and sentenced to prison. Chambers (D) did not take a direct appeal from these convictions, but applied for a writ of habeas corpus. After state and federal appeals courts denied granting the writ, the U.S. Supreme Court granted certiorari.

ISSUE: Is a warrantless search of an automobile permissible where there is probable cause to believe that the vehicle is carrying evidence and fruits of the crime, and the car itself is seized and held without a warrant for whatever period is necessary to obtain a warrant for search?

HOLDING AND DECISION: (White, J.) Yes. The warrantless search of an automobile is permissible where there is probable cause to believe that the vehicle is carrying evidence and fruits of the crime, and the car itself is seized and held without a warrant for whatever period is necessary to obtain a warrant for search. Automobiles may be searched without a warrant in circumstances where the intrusion would not be permissible for a house. The opportunity to search a car is fleeting since it is movable. Here, the station wagon could have been searched on the spot, since there was probable cause to search and it was a fleeting target for a search. Affirmed.

DISSENT: (Harlan, J.) Seizure of the car for the period necessary to enable the officers to obtain a warrant is the lesser intrusion, and therefore the more desirable action. The Court's approval of a warrantless search in this instance is not consistent with the Fourth Amendment's mandate of obedience to judicial procedure. This is so where the lesser intrusion is available.

EDITOR'S ANALYSIS: This case is in accord with the proposition that the Fourth Amendment is less strict with cars than it is with homes. The moveability of the car, the lesser aspect of privacy, and the plain view of the auto on the highway contribute to this.

[For more information on automobile searches, see Casenote Law Outline on Criminal Procedure, Chapter 8, Search Warrant Exception: Automobile Searches.]

NOTES:

CASENOTE LEGAL BRIEFS — CRIMINAL PROCEDURE

CALIFORNIA v. ACEVEDO
111 S. Ct. 1982 (1991).

NATURE OF CASE: Review of denial of motion to suppress evidence in a narcotics prosecution.

FACT SUMMARY: Police searched a container in Acevedo's (D) vehicle, despite a lack of probable cause to search the whole vehicle.

CONCISE RULE OF LAW: Police do not need probable cause to search an entire vehicle to search a container found therein.

FACTS: Police "staked out" the apartment of an individual known to have recently imported marijuana. Acevedo (D) was seen to enter this apartment and leave carrying a brown paper bag that appeared full. The police stopped his vehicle, opened his bag, and found marijuana. Acevedo (D) was prosecuted for possession. His motion to suppress was denied, and he plead guilty. On appeal, the California court of appeal held that the evidence should have been suppressed as the fruit of an illegal search. From this, the State (P) appealed and the Supreme Court granted certiorari.

ISSUE: Do police need probable cause to search an entire vehicle to search a container found therein?

HOLDING AND DECISION: (Blackmun, J.) No. Police do not need probable cause to search an entire vehicle to search a container found therein. This Court has held that police, if probable cause exists to search a vehicle, may search a closed container therein. However, the Court has also held that search of a container found requires a warrant, even if found in a vehicle. This distinction was based on the notion that a container carries a high expectation of privacy. In practice, however, numerous flaws in these rules have become evident. The line between probable cause to search a vehicle and probable cause to search only a container therein is fuzzy at best and has presented continuing confusion in law enforcement. Waste of law enforcement manpower has resulted, as police often elect to search an entire vehicle when they know or suspect that contraband is only in one container therein. Consequently, the legal dichotomy formulated by this Court has led to police being required to conduct a more intrusive search to justify a less intrusive one. Finally, the rule against opening containers not part of a general vehicle search in reality provides no significant protection of privacy, as police can impound the container and obtain a warrant. In view of these considerations, the better rule, adopted here, is that police may search an auto and any containers therein when they have probable cause to believe contraband is contained anywhere therein. Here, the police had probable cause to believe marijuana was in the paper bag, so the warrantless search was valid. Reversed.

CONCURRENCE: (Scalia, J.) The warrantless search of a closed container, outside a privately-owned building, is reasonable under the Fourth Amendment as long as there is probable cause.

DISSENT: (Stevens, J.) When authorities have probable cause to believe that a closed container conceals incriminating materials, and this container is placed in an automobile, they may seize, but not search, this container until a warrant has been issued.

EDITOR'S ANALYSIS: Most searches require a warrant; for the most part, warrantless searches are per se invalid. Autos and movable containers are the exception to the rule because of their movability. The Supreme Court has been trying for many years to define the limits of warrantless searches in this area, the present case being such an effort.

[For more information on the warrantless search of an automobile, see Casenote Law Outline on Criminal Procedure, Chapter 8, § I, General Rules.]

NOTES:

PAYTON v. NEW YORK
445 U.S. 573 (1980).

NATURE OF CASE: Consolidated appeals from convictions for murder.

FACT SUMMARY: Prior to attempting to arrest Payton (D) in his home, police failed to obtain an arrest warrant.

CONCISE RULE OF LAW: Police may not enter a person's home to make a routine felony arrest without a warrant.

FACTS: Police detectives, believing that they had sufficient evidence to link Payton (D) to a murder, went to his apartment. When no one answered their knock, they broke down the door. No one was home, but an incriminating bullet casing was found. Payton (D) later surrendered and was tried for murder. The casing was admitted over Payton's (D) objection. He was convicted, and the New York Court of Appeals affirmed. The Supreme Court granted review of Payton's (D) case and that of one Riddick (D), which presented a similar situation.

ISSUE: May police enter a person's home to make a routine felony arrest without a warrant?

HOLDING AND DECISION: (Stevens, J.) No. Police may not enter a person's home to make a routine felony arrest without a warrant. Both in terms of its underlying principles and its literal terms, the Fourth Amendment gives a specially protected status to the home. Seizures of the person and seizures of property within a home are both protected by the Amendment from being unreasonably effected. Consequently, just as police may not effect a routine search of a premises without a warrant, they cannot make a routine arrest therein without a warrant. Here, as the would-be arrest of Payton (D) presented no exigent circumstances, a warrant should have been obtained. Reversed.

DISSENT: (White, J.) It has long been held that public arrest does not require a warrant. Surely an arrest made in the home constitutes no greater humiliation, particularly in light of the common law requirements of knocking first and announcing the intent to arrest.

EDITOR'S ANALYSIS: The consequences of an unlawful arrest relate more to evidence than actual apprehension. Searches of a home or the person may be effected pursuant to a lawful arrest. If the arrest turns out to have been unlawful, any evidence found pursuant to the arrest is rendered inadmissible.

NOTES:

[For more information on arrests in the home, see Casenote Law Outline on Criminal Procedure, Chapter 4, § II, Warrants: In-Home Arrests.]

CAMARA v. MUNICIPAL COURT OF THE CITY & COUNTY OF SAN FRANCISCO
387 U.S. 523 (1967).

NATURE OF CASE: Review of denial of petition for writ of prohibition.

FACT SUMMARY: Camara (P) contended that routine housing and building code inspections required a search warrant.

CONCISE RULE OF LAW: Routine housing and building code inspections require a search warrant.

FACTS: Camara (P) on several occasions refused to admit housing inspectors, engaged in routine housing and building code inspections, into his apartment. A criminal complaint was filed against him. When his demurrer was overruled, he petitioned the court of appeals for a writ of prohibition, contending that he was not required to admit the inspectors without a warrant. The petition was denied, and the Supreme Court granted review.

ISSUE: Do routine housing and building code inspections require a search warrant?

HOLDING AND DECISION: (White, J.) Yes. Routine housing and building code inspections require a search warrant. Whether government officials wish to search a person's home for evidence of a penal code violation or merely for evidence of noncompliance with administrative regulations does not greatly matter in a Fourth Amendment analysis. Even the most law-abiding citizen has an interest in limiting the circumstances under which his home may be invaded by official authority. To hold that administrative inspections do not require warrants would leave with officials unbridled discretion with respect to when to invade a home, which is the very thing the Fourth Amendment was adopted to prevent. While government does have an interest in ensuring that its regulations are obeyed, it has not been suggested that a warrant requirement would prevent achievement of this goal. Therefore, a warrant must be required for official inspections. [The Court went on to discuss the circumstances under which a warrant might issue. The Court held that an area inspection is reasonable under the Fourth Amendment and that probable cause could be shown through statistical evidence of the likelihood of a violation.] Reversed.

EDITOR'S ANALYSIS: The probable cause requirement permitted here would never be sufficient in a criminal search. The main reasons for the looser standard are pragmatic. Both a history of public acceptance of housing inspections and the public interest in enforcement made the standard acceptable.

NOTES:

[For more information on administrative searches, see Casenote Law Outline on Criminal Procedure, Chapter 13, § I, Administrative Code Inspections.]

TERRY v. OHIO
392 U.S. 1 (1968).

NATURE OF CASE: Review of order denying motion to suppress in prosecution for carrying concealed weapons.

FACT SUMMARY: Terry (D), subject to a "frisk" by a police officer, contended that such a procedure could not have been performed absent probable cause to arrest.

CONCISE RULE OF LAW: Police may stop and frisk an individual whom they reasonably suspect may be armed and dangerous, even if probable cause to arrest is not present.

FACTS: McFadden, a police detective of 35 years' experience, was patrolling his beat on foot when he observed Terry (D) and another man repeatedly strolling by a store, looking in, and then walking away. This continued for over 10 minutes. McFadden formed the opinion that they were casing the store. He approached them and asked for identification. When their responses proved evasive, McFadden spun Terry (D) against a wall. Frisking him, he found a gun. Terry (D) was charged with carrying a concealed weapon. His motion to suppress was denied, and the state supreme court affirmed. The U.S. Supreme Court granted review.

ISSUE: May police stop and frisk an individual whom they reasonably suspect may be armed and dangerous, even if probable cause to arrest is not present?

HOLDING AND DECISION: (Warren, C.J.) Yes. Police may stop and frisk an individual whom they reasonably suspect may be armed and dangerous, even if probable cause to arrest is not present. Competing values are at issue here. On the one hand, the rapidly increasing dangerousness on city streets has created the need for flexible responses on the part of law enforcement. On the other hand is the argument that the authority of the police to search a person must be limited to situations where probable cause is present for the Fourth Amendment to have any meaning. Superimposed on this analysis is the limited ability of the judiciary to control day-to-day situations on city streets. The exclusionary rule can only go so far in controlling police conduct. When it cannot do so, its reasons for existence cease. The point of departure for analysis is that the Fourth Amendment's reasonableness requirement remains central. The reasonableness of a stop and frisk depends upon weighing the governmental interest in police and bystander security against a possibly armed criminal and every citizen's interest against police interference. This Court believes that a proper balance between these interests is struck by a rule allowing the minimally intrusive stop and frisk for weapons when an officer suspects, on an objectively reasonable level, that a person may be armed and dangerous. Here, Terry's (D) conduct was sufficiently suggestive of an intent to rob that McFadden's belief in this regard was reasonable. The stop, therefore, did not constitute a Fourth Amendment violation. Affirmed.

CONCURRENCE: (Harlan, J.) Once circumstances justify a confrontation with a citizen, the right to frisk naturally flows therefrom.

CONCURRENCE: (White, J.) A person cannot be compelled to cooperate if addressed by an officer, and such refusal cannot in itself furnish a basis for arrest.

DISSENT: (Douglas, J.) Nothing less than probable cause can justify forcible detention of an individual.

EDITOR'S ANALYSIS: The exclusionary rule is found nowhere in the Constitution. It was created by the Court as a prophylactic measure to advance the rights found in the Fourth Amendment. In the present case, the Court reasoned that when the rule could no longer serve its prophylactic purpose, which it believed to be the case here, it should not be imposed.

[For more information on "stop and frisk," see Casenote Law Outline on Criminal Procedure, Chapter 12, § I, Terry v. Ohio: The Case.]

NOTES:

CHIMEL v. CALIFORNIA
395 U.S. 752 (1969).

NATURE OF CASE: Review of burglary conviction.

FACT SUMMARY: After lawfully arresting Chimel (D) for burglary, the police searched his entire house incident to the arrest.

CONCISE RULE OF LAW: A search incident to a lawful arrest cannot be of unlimited scope.

FACTS: Police obtained an arrest warrant for Chimel (D) for a burglary of a coin shop. Police went to his residence and were admitted by Chimel's (D) wife. When he came home from work, Chimel (D) was arrested. Police then searched his entire home, finding incriminating evidence in various rooms. At trial, Chimel's (D) suppression motion, based on the unlimited scope of the search, was denied. He was convicted, and the conviction was affirmed on appeal. The Supreme Court granted review.

ISSUE: Can a search warrant incident to a lawful arrest be unlimited in scope?

HOLDING AND DECISION: (Stewart, J.) No. A search incident to a lawful arrest cannot be of unlimited scope. The Fourth Amendment was a reaction to the hated general warrants imposed upon the colonists by the British government. The Amendment places specific limits on search warrants, mandating constraints on the scope of searches thereunder. It would be entirely inconsistent with the intent behind the Amendment to allow a search incident to an arrest be of unlimited scope. When an arrest is made, it is reasonable for the arresting officer to search the arrestee's person for weapons or other dangerous objects. It is likewise reasonable to allow a search of the arrestee's immediate area. However, to allow a general search of an arrestee's home goes far beyond any legitimate justification for a search incident to an arrest. Here, the scope of the search involved Chimel's (D) entire house, so the search was contrary to the Fourth and Fourteenth Amendments. Reversed.

DISSENT: (White, J.) When a person is arrested in his house, probable cause to search the entire house will almost always exist. To impose a warrant requirement on arresting police to search the house places an unreasonable burden on law enforcement.

EDITOR'S ANALYSIS: Prior to this case, the scope of a search incident to arrest had never been clearly defined. A series of cases dating back to 1914 had recognized this exception to the warrant requirement but had never delineated how far the exception went. This issue was settled by the present decision.

[For more information on scope of search incident to arrest, see Casenote Law Outline on Criminal Procedure, Chapter 7, § II, Scope of the Warrant Exception: In General.]

NOTES:

UNITED STATES v. ROBINSON
414 U.S. 218 (1973).

NATURE OF CASE: Review of grant of motion to suppress evidence in prosecution for narcotics possession.

FACT SUMMARY: Robinson (D) was subjected to a full search of the person following a lawful arrest for narcotics possession.

CONCISE RULE OF LAW: Police may conduct a full search of the person following a lawful arrest.

FACTS: Robinson (D) was seen by Jenks, a police officer, to be driving an automobile. Knowing from a previous encounter that Robinson's (D) operator's license had expired, Jenks pulled him over. Finding the license to be expired, Jenks arrested Robinson (D) for driving without a license, a misdemeanor under District of Columbia law. Jenks then searched Robinson's (D) person and found a cigarette package. Opening the package, he found vials of what proved to be heroin. Robinson (D) wa charged with a narcotics law violation. The district court denied his motion to suppress, but the D.C. Circuit reversed en banc, holding the scope of the search to have been excessive. The Supreme Court granted review.

ISSUE: May police conduct a full search of the person following a lawful arrest?

HOLDING AND DECISION: (Rehnquist, J.) Yes. Police may conduct a full search of the person following a lawful arrest. That an officer may search a suspect following an arrest is without question. What has not always been clear is the permissible scope of such a search. The court of appeals here was of the view that a search going beyond an attempt to locate a weapon was unreasonable. This is a flawed analysis. Once an arrest has been effected, a reasonable intrusion of the arrestee has by definition occurred; a subsequent full search constitutes no greater intrusion. Beyond this, the governmental interest in such a situation goes beyond the officer's safety. It has a legitimate interest in obtaining evidence. For these reasons, the rule imposed by the court of appeals was erroneous. Reversed.

DISSENT: (Marshall, J.) No formula exists for what constitutes a reasonable search. The per se rule enunciated by the Court here violates this principle. In the context of this case, search of the cigarette pack was unreasonable.

EDITOR'S ANALYSIS: The court of appeals in this case felt constrained to follow Terry v. Ohio, 392 U.S. 1 (1968). Terry had held that a detainee could be frisked for weapons but could not be subjected to a full search. The prime difference between Terry and the present case was the existence of probable cause in the latter, something the court of appeals placed less emphasis upon than the Supreme Court. Still one must wonder what evidence of driving without a license could be found beyond the lack of a license or possession of an expired license.

NOTES:

NEW YORK v. BELTON
453 U.S. 454 (1981).

NATURE OF CASE: Appeal from exclusion of evidence.

FACT SUMMARY: After stopping a car for speeding, police, who smelled marijuana smoke in the car, found marijuana on the floor of the car and, after arresting the occupants, searched the pockets of Belton's (D) jacket in the back seat, there finding cocaine.

CONCISE RULE OF LAW: When police have made a lawful custodial arrest of the occupant of an automobile, they may, as a contemporaneous incident of that arrest, search the passenger compartment of the automobile.

FACTS: Belton (D) and others were traveling on the New York State Thruway at an excessive rate of speed in an automobile. A state trooper in an unmarked police car pulled the vehicle over and smelled marijuana smoke. He determined that none of the four occupants owned the car. He also noticed an envelope marked "Supergold" on the floor of the car. He arrested the four men and examined the envelope which contained marijuana. He then searched the back seat of the car, having removed the men to the police vehicle, and unzipped the pocket of Belton's (D) jacket lying there. It contained cocaine. The trial court denied Belton's (D) motion to suppress the cocaine but the New York Court of Appeals reversed. The United States Supreme Court granted certiorari.

ISSUE: When police have made a lawful custodial arrest of the occupant of an automobile, may they, as a contemporaneous incident of that arrest, search the passenger compartment of the automobile?

HOLDING AND DECISION: (Stewart, J.) Yes. No straight forward rule has emerged regarding the proper scope of a search of the interior of an automobile incident to a lawful custodial arrest of its occupants. In Chimel v. California, this court held that a search of the passenger compartment of an automobile is justified because it is within the reach of the arrestee, who may reach somewhere within that area to grab a weapon. The jacket, in this case, was in the passenger compartment of the car, where Belton (D) had just been located and could have had immediate access before he was removed. When police have made a lawful custodial arrest of the occupant of an automobile, they may, as a contemporaneous incident of that arrest, search the passenger compartment of the automobile. Reversed.

DISSENT: (Brennan, J.) The Court turns back today on the careful analysis produced by Chimel v. California and applies an arbitrary rule extending to recent occupants of automobiles. This rule fails to reflect the policy behind Chimel. While in Chimel the arrestee was within reach of the area searched at the time of the arrest, Belton (D), in this case, was handcuffed in a patrol car while the passenger compartment of the car in which he had been riding was searched. The upholding of this search is a wholesale retreat from this court's carefully developed search-incident-to-arrest analysis.

EDITOR'S ANALYSIS: The underlying policy for permitting the search of an area within the control of an arrestee was the protection of the arresting officers from the arrestee, who might grab a weapon and attack. A further justification announced in Chimel v. California was the possibility that the arrestee may quickly reach for and destroy a small piece of evidence. Neither of these reasons is furthered by the Belton rule, which squares neither with constitutional law history nor Justice Stewart's own opinion in Robbins v. California.

[For more information on automobile searches incident to an arrest, see Casenote Law Outline on Criminal Procedure, Chapter 7, § III, Special Rule: Search of an Automobile Incident to an Arrest.]

NOTES:

COLORADO v. BERTINE
479 U.S. 367 (1987).

NATURE OF CASE: Appeal of order to suppress evidence.

FACT SUMMARY: A routine inventory of Bertine's (D) auto after Bertine's (D) DUI arrest produced closed containers which, when opened, revealed contraband.

CONCISE RULE OF LAW: A police inventory inspection may involve the opening of closed containers.

FACTS: Bertine (D) was arrested for drunk driving. Following the arrest, Bertine's (D) auto was inventoried. Sealed containers were found which, when opened, revealed illegal drugs. Bertine (D) moved to suppress the contents of the containers. The trial court granted the motion on state constitutional grounds. The state supreme court upheld the suppression, but on federal constitutional grounds. The State (P) appealed.

ISSUE: May a police inventory inspection involve the opening of closed containers?

HOLDING AND DECISION: (Rehnquist, C.J.) Yes. A police inventory inspection may involve the opening of closed containers. Inventory searches are a well-defined exception to the Fourth Amendment's warrant requirement, and probable cause does not figure into the analysis, provided that the inspection was in fact routine and not a subterfuge for a criminal investigation. The state has a legitimate interest in ensuring against theft and fraudulent claims of property loss, and, therefore, an inventory is proper. It is not possible to know the contents of a closed container without opening it, so the opening of a closed container during inventory is proper. Reversed.

CONCURRENCE: (Blackmun, J.) The opening of a closed container is permissible only if done as part of routine procedures mandating such opening every time.

DISSENT: (Marshall, J.) The procedure here afforded the police officer excessive discretion.

EDITOR'S ANALYSIS: The police department in this instance had at least two options, one being simply to park and lock the vehicle in a public area. The police chose to impound and search the vehicle instead. The dissent argued that this, in effect, gave the police discretion regarding whether to search.

NOTES:

[For more information on inventory inspection, see Casenote Law Outline on Criminal Procedure, Chapter 10, § I, Automobile Inventories.]

DELAWARE v. PROUSE
440 U.S. 648 (1979).

NATURE OF CASE: Review of grant of motion to suppress evidence in prosecution for narcotics possession.

FACT SUMMARY: Prouse (D) was charged with marijuana possession after a random check of his driver's license revealed the drug in plain view in his car.

CONCISE RULE OF LAW: Authorities may not conduct random checks of drivers' licenses and registrations.

FACTS: A county patrol officer pulled Prouse (D) over to check his driver's license and vehicle registration. This was done on a purely random, chance basis. After the vehicle stopped, the officer saw marijuana in plain view in the car. Prouse (D) was arrested and charged with possession. The trial court granted a motion to suppress, agreeing that the stop violated the Fourth Amendment. The Delaware Supreme Court affirmed. The Supreme Court granted review.

ISSUE: May authorities conduct random checks of drivers' licenses and registrations?

HOLDING AND DECISION: (White, J.) No. Authorities may not conduct random checks of drivers' licenses and registrations. There can be no question but that random, discretionary license checks implicate the Fourth Amendment, involving as they do interference with liberty, consumption of time, and probable anxiety. The proffered justification for such checks is highway safety. However, it seems clear that random license checks are hardly an efficient means to secure such safety. Vehicle stops for violations of traffic rules and auto safety equipment have historically been much more productive in ensuring highway safety and are much less intrusive under the Fourth Amendment. Therefore, random license checks cannot survive Fourth Amendment scrutiny. Reversed.

CONCURRENCE: (Blackmun, J.) Spot checks that do not involve unrestrained discretion may be constitutionally acceptable.

DISSENT: (Rehnquist, J.) It has been established that police may institute roadblock-type spot checks. Why those should be considered valid but not the sort of check at issue here is a question not answered.

EDITOR'S ANALYSIS: It appears that the key element in the Court's analysis was the unbridled discretion involved in this case. An officer being able to stop a car for no reason other than whim smacks of Orwell. Presumably, some sort of spot-check system not permitting such discretion would be valid, if limited perhaps to vehicle safety concerns.

NOTES:

MICHIGAN DEPARTMENT OF STATE POLICE v. SITZ
110 S. Ct. 2481 (1990).

NATURE OF CASE: Review of order invalidating a police sobriety checkpoint program.

FACT SUMMARY: A program of random sobriety checkpoints on public highways was challenged as unconstitutional.

CONCISE RULE OF LAW: A state may institute random sobriety checkpoints on highways.

FACTS: The Michigan State Police (D) instituted a program wherein roving patrols of officers set up roadblocks and checked passing cars for intoxicated drivers. Sitz (P) challenged this program as violative of the Fourth Amendment. The Michigan Court of Appeals so held and struck down the program. The Supreme Court granted review.

ISSUE: May a state institute random sobriety checkpoints on highways?

HOLDING AND DECISION: (Rehnquist, C.J.) Yes. A state may institute random sobriety checkpoints on highways. The validity of such a program depends upon a consideration of the relevant state interest, the intrusion upon individual privacy, and the effectiveness of the program in achieving its goal. Here, there can be no disputing that states have a heavy interest in stopping drunk driving. The intrusion, which involves the stopping of a vehicle and a brief interview, is no more than minor. The effectiveness of the program is not demonstrably absolute; however, it is not the function of this Court to tell the political branches of government which of several methods which may be used to achieve a goal must be used. As long as there is some connection between goal and result, which here there is, the selected method will not be invalid for lack of effectiveness. For these reasons, the program was valid. Reversed.

DISSENT: (Brennan, J.) As intoxicated drivers can be identified by erratic driving, an individualized determination should be required.

DISSENT: (Stevens, J.) Mobile checkpoints, unlike permanent ones, constitute a significant intrusion into personal privacy.

EDITOR'S ANALYSIS: The nearest antecedent to this case was United States v. Martinez-Fuerte, 428 U.S. 543 (1976). In that action, a permanent nonborder random immigration checkpoint was upheld as constitutional. Justice Stevens felt the two cases to be dissimilar, as borne out by his dissent, because immigration checkpoints were fixed in place, while drunk driving checkpoints were mobile. Also, the problems to be countered were quite different in nature.

NOTES:

YBARRA v. ILLINOIS
444 U.S. 85 (1979).

NATURE OF CASE: Review of conviction for narcotics possession.

FACT SUMMARY: Ybarra (D), a patron of a tavern, was searched pursuant to a search warrant authorizing search of the premises.

CONCISE RULE OF LAW: A person incidentally on premises subject to a search warrant may not be searched absent independent probable cause therefor.

FACTS: Police, having obtained a warrant to search a tavern whose proprietor was suspected of possessing drugs, entered the tavern. They proceeded to "pat down" most patrons, including Ybarra (D). The pat-down produced a cigarette package containing what proved to be heroin. Ybarra (D) was convicted of possession, his suppression motion having been denied. The conviction was affirmed, and the Supreme Court granted review.

ISSUE: May a person incidentally on premises subject to a search warrant be searched absent independent probable cause therefor?

HOLDING AND DECISION: (Stewart, J.) No. A person incidentally on premises subject to a search warrant may not be searched absent independent probable cause therefor. A person's mere propinquity to others suspected of criminal activity does not, without more, give rise to probable cause to search or seize that individual. Such proximity does not even give rise to a reasonable suspicion to pat down an individual, absent some independent reason to believe he may be armed. In this case, nothing in the record demonstrates that Ybarra (D) did anything suspicious that might have given an officer reason to believe he presented a danger. Therefore, even the mild "stop and frisk" standard was not met in this case, to say nothing of the more stringent probable cause standard. For this reason, the pat-down constituted a Fourth and Fourteenth Amendment violation. Reversed.

DISSENT: (Burger, C.J.) The standard imposed by the Court here would require searching officers to ignore the possibility that those present in an establishment suspected of trading in narcotics might be dangerous. The Fourth Amendment does not require such foolhardiness on the part of the police.

EDITOR'S ANALYSIS: The "stop and frisk" standard analysis was articulated in the case Terry v. Ohio, 392 U.S. 1 (1968). In that case, it was held that a suspect could be frisked, under certain conditions, without probable cause. The Court here declined to extend the Terry rule, which remains a fairly narrow exception to the warrant requirement.

NOTES:

MICHIGAN v. SUMMERS
452 U.S. 692 (1981).

NATURE OF CASE: Review of order dismissing criminal charges.

FACT SUMMARY: Summers (D), who was detained during an authorized search of his house, was arrested when contraband was discovered therein.

CONCISE RULE OF LAW: Occupants of a house being searched pursuant to a warrant may be detained during the search.

FACTS: Police obtained a warrant to search Summers' (D) house, believing contraband to be contained therein. When they arrived, Summers (D) was outside the house, in the process of leaving. The police detained him while they searched his house. Finding mild narcotics inside, they arrested him. A search of his person uncovered a package of heroin. Summers (D) was charged with heroin possession. The trial court granted a motion to suppress the heroin, ruling that Summers' (D) detention had violated the Fourth Amendment. This was affirmed on appeal. The Supreme Court granted review.

ISSUE: May occupants of a house being searched pursuant to a warrant be detained during the search?

HOLDING AND DECISION: (Stevens, J.) Yes. Occupants of a house being searched pursuant to a warrant may be detained during the search. Some seizures admittedly implicating the Fourth Amendment may be made on less than probable cause, if substantial law enforcement interests are at stake. A search of a person's home pursuant to a warrant is a significant intrusion into his privacy. Detention of that person in the home adds no greater intrusion. On the law-enforcement-necessity side of the equation, it is quite conceivable that a search of a home may lead to violent behavior or some other danger to police officers if occupants are not detained. These considerations result in the conclusion that a detention of an occupant on less than probable cause is reasonable under the Fourth Amendment. Reversed.

DISSENT: (Stewart, J.) The balancing test employed by the Court constitutes an improper Fourth Amendment analysis. The Amendment's probable cause requirement is the point of balance between police objectives and personal privacy.

EDITOR'S ANALYSIS: Prior to this case, the Court's exceptions to the probable cause requirement were fairly rare. Probably the most well-known example of these exceptions was that articulated in Terry v. Ohio, 392 U.S. 1 (1968). This case permitted police to stop and frisk a person on reasonable suspicion rather than probable cause. Another example was United States v. Brignon-Prince, 422 U.S. 873 (1975), which allowed roving border inspections on less than probable cause.

[For more information on auto searches, see Casenote Law Outline on Criminal Procedure, Chapter 7, § I, General Rules.]

NOTES:

NEW YORK v. CLASS
475 U.S. 106 (1986).

NATURE OF CASE: Review of reversal of conviction of illegal possession of a weapon.

FACT SUMMARY: A police officer, while looking for the identification number of Class' (D) vehicle, noticed a gun under the seat.

CONCISE RULE OF LAW: Contraband discovered pursuant to a search for a vehicle identification number may be constitutionally seized.

FACTS: Police pulled over Class (D) for speeding and having a broken windshield. An officer looked through the windshield for the vehicle identification number. Seeing that it was covered by papers on the dashboard, he opened the door to remove the papers. Upon doing this, the officer noticed a gun under the driver's seat. Class (D) was arrested. He was charged with illegal possession of a weapon, tried, and convicted. The New York Court of Appeals reversed, holding that the officer's entry into the vehicle violated the Fourth Amendment. The Supreme Court granted review.

ISSUE: May a contraband discovered pursuant to a search for a vehicle identification number be constitutionally seized?

HOLDING AND DECISION: (O'Connor, J.) Yes. Contraband discovered pursuant to a search for a vehicle identification number (VIN) may be constitutionally seized. "Reasonableness" of a search under the Fourth Amendment requires balancing of the need to conduct a search against the invasion of privacy which the search entails. A VIN is a significant thread in the web of automobile regulation. The ability of officers to gain access to it is very important in the prevention of auto theft and the resultant property and loss of life that may result therefrom. Consequently, the need for access to VINs is great. On the other side of the test, the VIN is displayed in vehicles in a location that can be viewed from the outside. A person has no privacy interest in the outside of his vehicle, so he has no privacy interest in his VIN. He cannot artificially create such an interest by concealing the VIN. Consequently, if an officer must enter the auto to uncover the VIN, he may do so. Any contraband found incidentally to this limited search may be lawfully seized. Here, the officer entered the vehicle to uncover the VIN, and his finding of the gun was incidental thereto. It was, therefore, property admitted into evidence. Reversed.

CONCURRENCE: (Powell, J.) The Court's analysis can be stated simply by saying that the officer's efforts to inspect the VIN were reasonable.

DISSENT: (Brennan, J.) The Court improperly focuses on the object of the officer's search — the VIN — rather than the search itself. The object of a search does not alter the probable cause requirement for auto searches.

EDITOR'S ANALYSIS: Autos, because of their inherent mobility and pervasive regulation, are treated differently under the Fourth Amendment than are homes. A notable embodiment of this principle can be found in California v. Carney, 471 U.S. 386 (1985). That case held that a motor home could be searched without a warrant, provided probable cause existed to do so. It would seem that a search warrant would be required to search a "mobile home" that is permanently fixed to a foundation because the question of inherent mobility could not be raised in such circumstance.

[For more information on searches of autos, see Casenote Law Outline on Criminal Procedure, Chapter 8, § I, General Rules.]

NOTES:

ZURCHER v. STANFORD DAILY
436 U.S. 547 (1978).

NATURE OF CASE: Review of injunctive and declaratory relief granted pursuant to 42 U.S.C. § 1983.

FACT SUMMARY: Police obtained a search warrant to search the offices of the Stanford Daily (P) for evidence of a crime it reported.

CONCISE RULE OF LAW: A warrant may be issued to search a nonsuspect's property for evidence of a crime without the authorities having first attempted to subpoena the evidence.

FACTS: A photographer for the Stanford Daily (P) observed and photographed an assault upon police by demonstrators protesting at Stanford University. When the Stanford Daily (D) published an article with photographs about the assault, local police obtained a warrant to search the Daily's (P) office for other photos. None were found. The Stanford Daily (P) subsequently filed a civil rights action under 42 U.S.C. § 1983, seeking injunctive and declaratory relief. The District Court held that a warrant could issue to search a nonsuspect's property only if an attempted subpoena had failed to produce results. An injunction against further searches was issued. The Ninth Circuit affirmed, and the Supreme Court granted review.

ISSUE: May a warrant be issued to search a nonsuspect's property for evidence of a crime without the authorities having first attempted to subpoena the evidence?

HOLDING AND DECISION: (White, J.) Yes. A warrant may be issued to search a nonsuspect's property for evidence of a crime without the authorities having first attempted to subpoena the evidence. The position taken by the District Court here is without precedent. Rather, the authorities are quire clear that the grounds for issuing a warrant to search property are the same whether or not the owner of the property is implicated in the relevant crime. This is only logical, as the state's interest in recovering evidence of a crime is the same no matter who owns the property to be searched. The problems with first requiring a subpoena are obvious. Once the subpoena is received, the wrongdoer, who will most likely have some level of access to the premises on which the evidence is located, will have ample time to hide it away. Further, since subpoenas are much easier to obtain than warrants, it is very likely that a prosecutor will resort to a warrant only when he is confident that a subpoena will not suffice. For these reasons, as a general rule, a subpoena is not a condition precedent to the search of a nonsuspect's property. Here, the Stanford Daily (P) argues that media outlets require heightened protection under the First Amendment. However, this Court believes that the protections of the Fourth Amendment are sufficient to protect the press from unjustified intrusion. Reversed.

CONCURRENCE: (Powell, J.) It would be quite difficult to decide on a case-by-case basis when a subpoena could serve as an adequate substitute for subpoena.

DISSENT: (Stevens, J.) Completely innocent parties may, through no voluntary act of their own, possess evidence of a crime. The intrusion upon these persons' liberty by announced police searches is serious.

EDITOR'S ANALYSIS: The issue here can find its ultimate genesis in the case Warden v. Hayden, 387 U.S. 294 (1967). Prior to that case, many courts held that a warrant could issue to search for only contraband or instrumentalities of a crime. Warden held that a warrant could issue for any evidence. Consequently, as innocent third parties would be much more likely to have evidence as opposed to contraband, their being targets of a search became much more likely.

NOTES:

TENNESSEE v. GARNER
471 U.S. 1 (1985).

NATURE OF CASE: Review of order reversing defense verdict in federal civil rights action.

FACT SUMMARY: Tennessee's (D) law permitting the use of deadly force to apprehend any fleeing felony suspect was challenged as unconstitutional.

CONCISE RULE OF LAW: Deadly force may not be used to apprehend a fleeing felony suspect unless there is probable cause to believe that the suspect poses a significant threat to the safety of others.

FACTS: Tennessee (D) state law permitted police officers to use deadly force to stop any fleeing felony suspect. At one point, Edward Garner, suspected of having just burglarized a house, was shot and killed while attempting to flee. He was unarmed and gave no appearance thereof. Garner (P), his father, brought an action for damages in district court under 42 U.S.C. § 1983, contending that the officer's acts violated his son's civil rights. The district court held the Tennessee (D) law constitutional and entered a defense verdict. The court of appeals reversed, and the Supreme Court granted review.

ISSUE: May deadly force be used to apprehend a fleeing suspect if there is no probable cause to believe that the suspect poses a significant threat to the safety of others?

HOLDING AND DECISION: (White, J.) No. Deadly force may not be used to apprehend a fleeing suspect unless there is probable cause to believe that the suspect poses a significant threat to the safety of others. Apprehension of a suspect is a "seizure" covered by the Fourth Amendment. The reasonableness of any seizure thereunder involves the balancing of the individual's personal interests against those of the government. With respect to deadly force, the individual's interest in remaining alive is obvious. The government's interest in effective law enforcement is equally clear. Deadly force does not always advance this interest. First, it can interfere with judicial determination of guilt or innocence. Also, statistics show that successful apprehensions are not noticeably higher in states that allow use of deadly force than in those that do not. It is true that, at common law, deadly force could be used to apprehend any felony suspect. However, at common law, all felonies were punishable by death, so killing a fleeing suspect was more commensurate with the ultimate punishment. Such is not the case today. In summation, only when a suspect poses significant threat to the safety of others is governmental interest in apprehension so great as to warrant deadly force. Here, the decedent did not pose such a threat, so deadly force was not warranted. Affirmed.

EDITOR'S ANALYSIS: In early times, felonies were limited to certain very serious crimes, such as murder, burglary, and rape, and were always punishable by death. Today, a felony is usually defined by the amount of time in prison one can receive for committing the crime, usually one or two years, depending upon the jurisdiction. Consequently, as societal attitudes toward the nature and degree of punishment have changed over the centuries, the Court did not feel constrained to incorporate the common law in existence at the time of the Fourth Amendment's adoption into its analysis.

[For more information on apprehension, see Casenote Law Outline on Criminal Procedure, Chapter 2, § X, "Seizure": Of Persons.]

NOTES:

SCHNECKLOTH v. BUSTAMONTE
412 U.S. 218 (1973).

NATURE OF CASE: Review of grant of federal writ of habeas corpus.

FACT SUMMARY: Bustamonte (P) contended that consent to search an automobile had not been voluntary because the person giving consent had not been told that he had a right to decline consent.

CONCISE RULE OF LAW: To be voluntary, consent to a search need not include a police admonition that consent may be withheld.

FACTS: Police stopped an auto for having a nonfunctioning headlight. The only occupant with a license, Alcala, informed the police that it was his brother's car. The officer asked if he could search the car. Alcala consented and cooperated in opening the trunk and glove compartment. Inside, certain forged checks were found. Bustamonte (P), a passenger, was charged with possessing a check with intent to defraud. He moved to suppress the checks, contending that consent to search had not been voluntary. The motion was denied, and he was convicted. This was affirmed on appeal. Bustamonte (P) filed a habeas corpus action. The district court denied the writ, but the Ninth Circuit reversed, holding that for a search consent to be voluntary, the consenting party had to be informed that consent could be withheld. The Supreme Court granted review.

ISSUE: To be voluntary, must consent to a search include a police admonition that consent may be withheld?

HOLDING AND DECISION: (Stewart, J.) No. To be voluntary, consent to a search need not include a police admonition that consent may be withheld. The notion of "voluntariness" is vague at best, and what exactly constitutes voluntary action will largely depend upon a person's philosophical perspective. In light of the difficulty in quantifying the meaning of voluntariness, the best approach in deciding whether it exists is on a case-by-case basis, examining all relevant factors, such as environment and level of coercion. No single criterion should be controlling. It is true that in some areas a "knowing" waiver is required, such as a waiver of counsel or custodial interrogation. However, these are situations in which the fairness of a trial is implicated. A Fourth Amendment search simply does not raise the implications of an unfair trial as does an absence of counsel or the circumstances of custodial interrogation. Consequently, no hard test for ascertaining voluntariness is appropriate. Here, the trial court's finding that Alcala's consent was voluntary appears to be supported by substantial evidence. Reversed.

DISSENT: (Marshall, J.) Consent involves a choice by a person to forgo his right to be free from police intrusion. Such a decision cannot realistically be called "choice" if the actor doesn't know he has the right to withhold consent.

EDITOR'S ANALYSIS: The basic Fourth Amendment principle is that a search requires a warrant. When a search involved not a warrant but consent, it is up to the prosecution to prove consent. What was at issue in the present case was what must be demonstrated to prove consent.

[For more information on voluntariness of consent, see Casenote Law Outline on Criminal Procedure, Chapter 11, § II, Lawful Consent: The "Voluntariness" Principle.]

NOTES:

RAKAS v. ILLINOIS
439 U.S. 128 (1978).

NATURE OF CASE: Appeal from conviction for armed robbery.

FACT SUMMARY: Rakas (D), a passenger in a searched automobile, moved to suppress the rifle and shells seized in the car, but his motion was denied because he lacked standing.

CONCISE RULE OF LAW: Passengers in automobiles who have no claimed relation to the automobile or the property seized do not have standing simply because they were legitimately on the premises at the time of the search.

FACTS: Police officers stopped a car suspected of being the getaway car in a robbery. The police officers ordered the occupants of the car to get out so they could search it. The police recovered a box of rifle shells in the locked glove compartment and a sawed-off rifle under the front passenger seat. Rakas (D), a passenger in the vehicle, was charged with armed robbery. At trial, Rakas (D) moved to suppress the evidence on the grounds that the search violated the Fourth and Fourteenth Amendments. Rakas (D) conceded he was only a passenger, he was not the owner of the car, and he did not own the rifle or the shells. The trial court held that Rakas (D) lacked standing to seek suppression and denied the motion. Rakas (D) was convicted of armed robbery, the Illinois Court of Appeals affirmed the decision, and he appealed to the U.S. Supreme Court.

ISSUE: Do passengers in automobiles who have no claimed relation to the automobile or the property seized have standing simply because they were legitimately on the premises at the time of the search?

HOLDING AND DECISION: (Rehnquist, J.) No. Passengers in automobiles who have no claimed relation to the automobile or the property seized do not have standing simply because they were legitimately on the premises at the time of the search. Rakas (D) asserted no property or possessory interest in the automobile or in the property seized. The fact that Rakas (D) was "legitimately on the premises" in the sense that he was in the car with the permission of the owner is not determinative of whether he had a legitimate expectation of privacy in the particular areas of the automobile searched (glove compartment or area under the seat of the car). In these areas, passengers simply would not normally have a legitimate expectation of privacy. Affirmed.

DISSENT: (White, J.) The decision invites police to engage in patently unreasonable searches every time an automobile contains more than one occupant. Should something be found, only the owner of the vehicle or the item will have standing to seek suppression, and the evidence will presumably be usable against the other occupants.

EDITOR'S ANALYSIS: This decision places auto passengers in a "damned if they do, damned if they don't" position. If the passengers of the car admitted to owning the rifle and shells, they would then have standing to assert suppression. However, if they testified on their own behalf at trial, the prosecution could then impeach them as to their ownership of the rifle and shells on cross-examination.

[For more information on standing, see Casenote Law Outline on Criminal Procedure, Chapter 14, § II, Rakas v. Illinois.]

NOTES:

RAWLINGS v. KENTUCKY
448 U.S. 98 (1980).

NATURE OF CASE: Appeal from denial of a motion to suppress evidence in a prosecution for drug possession with intent to sell.

FACT SUMMARY: Rawlings (D) contended that he had standing to move to suppress drugs that he owned which were seized from a friend's purse by the police.

CONCISE RULE OF LAW: An evaluation of the totality of the circumstances will be made to determine whether an individual had a reasonable expectation of privacy in the place searched by the police.

FACTS: Rawlings (D) and Cox were staying at the house of a friend for whom the police had an arrest warrant. Upon the police's arrival, they noticed the smell of marijuana and saw marijuana seeds in the house and subsequently sought and obtained a warrant to search the premises. Prior to this, Rawlings (D) placed drugs in Cox's purse. Cox was required by the police to empty the contents of her purse onto a table. When the drugs fell out, Cox turned to Rawlings (D) and asked him to take what was his. He took the drugs, which were later introduced against him in a drug possession prosecution. Rawlings' (D) motion to suppress the drugs was denied, and he was found guilty of possession with intent to sell drugs. The Supreme Court of Kentucky affirmed, and Rawlings (D) appealed, arguing he had an expectation of privacy in the area searched.

ISSUE: Should an evaluation of the totality of the circumstances be made to determine whether an individual has a reasonable expectation of privacy?

HOLDING AND DECISION: (Rehnquist, J.) Yes. An evaluation of the totality of the circumstances will be made to determine whether an individual had a reasonable expectation of privacy. Such factors that could be considered are ownership of property seized and the location of the property at the time of the search. At the time Rawlings (D) dumped thousands of dollars worth of drugs into Cox's purse, he had known her only for a few days. Rawlings (D) had never had any prior access to Cox's purse, nor did he have the right to exclude other persons from having access to Cox's purse. Therefore, Rawlings (D) had no legitimate expectation of privacy in Cox's purse at the time of the search. Affirmed.

DISSENT: (Marshall, J.) This Court's holding cavalierly rejects the fundamental principle, unquestioned until this case, that an interest in either the place searched or the property seized is sufficient to invoke the Constitution's protections against unreasonable searches and seizures.

EDITOR'S ANALYSIS: The holding in this case has been widely criticized. By adding a "totality of the circumstances" test to the determination of whether one has a reasonable expectation of privacy in a certain place, a larger measure of uncertainty now arises. The determination becomes more subjective, and a person's own belief in the sense of privacy and personal security afforded when entrusting possessions to another is greatly weakened.

[For more information on standing, see Casenote Law Outline on Criminal Procedure, Chapter 14, § III, Where the Law Is Now.]

NOTES:

UNITED STATES v. CECCOLINI
435 U.S. 268 (1978).

NATURE OF CASE: Appeal from a suppression of a government witness' testimony.

FACT SUMMARY: The Government (P) contended that a witness' testimony was not obtained in violation of Ceccolini's (D) Fourth Amendment rights, even though an illegal search enabled the police to locate this witness.

CONCISE RULE OF LAW: In cases where an illegal search enables the police to locate a witness, the witness' statements will be less readily excluded as the fruit of illegal police conduct and a more direct link will be required before exclusion is allowed.

FACTS: A police officer entered Ceccolini's (D) place of business to talk with his friend, Hennessey. The officer, while talking with Hennessey, noticed an envelope with money sticking out lying on the cash register. Upon examining it, the officer saw that the envelope contained policy slips (betting forms) as well. After asking Hennessey to whom the envelope belonged, she replied that it belonged to Ceccolini (D), who asked her to give it to someone. The officer reported the night's events to the FBI, agents of which interviewed Hennessey four months later. Ceccolini (D) was summoned before a federal grand jury, where he testified that he had never taken policy bets at his store. Hennessey then testified to the contrary, and Ceccolini (D) was indicted for perjury. Ceccolini (D) moved to suppress Hennessey's testimony on the grounds that the illegal search enabled the police to find and interview her. The trial court granted Ceccolini's (D) motion to suppress Hennessey's testimony and found that without her testimony, there was insufficient evidence to support a guilty verdict. The court of appeals affirmed.

ISSUE: In cases where an illegal search enables police to locate a witness, should the witness' statements be less readily excludible as the fruit of illegal police conduct?

HOLDING AND DECISION: (Rehnquist, J.) Yes. In cases where an illegal search enables the police to locate a witness, a witness' statements will be less readily excluded as the fruit of illegal police conduct and a more direct link will be required before exclusion is allowed. The factors a court will consider include the extent to which the witness is willing to testify and the extent to which not allowing the witness to testify would deter future illegal police conduct. The evidence in this case indicated that Hennessey's testimony was of her own free will and in no way coerced or induced by official authority as a result of the officer's discovery of the policy slips. In addition, the slips were not used in questioning Hennessey. The cost of permanently silencing Hennessey would be too great for an evenhanded system of law enforcement to bear in order to secure such a speculative and every likely negligible deterrent effect. Reversed.

DISSENT: (Marshall, J.) The majority makes a point that "[t]he greater the willingness of the witness to testify . . . the smaller the incentive to conduct an illegal search to discover the witness." The premise of this statement is that the police refrain from illegal behavior in which they would otherwise engage when they know in advance both that a witness will be willing to testify and that he "will be discovered by legal means." This reasoning reverses the normal sequence of events. The instances must be very few in which a witness' willingness to testify is known before he is discovered.

EDITOR'S ANALYSIS: It should be noted that in its decision, the Court rejected the Government's (P) suggestion that it adopt what would in practice amount to a per se rule that the testimony of a live witness should not be excluded at trial no matter how close and proximate the connection between it and a violation of the Fourth Amendment. The Court instead used the "attenuated connection" principle established in Wong Sun v. United States, 371 U.S. 471 (1963), where evidence obtained by means sufficiently distinguishable from the original illegality is purged of the primary taint and therefore admissible.

[For more information on the fruit of the poisonous tree, see Casenote Law Outline on Criminal Procedure, Chapter 15, § V, "Fruit of the Poisonous Tree" Doctrine.]

NOTES:

UNITED STATES v. CREWS
445 U.S. 463 (1980).

NATURE OF CASE: Appeal from a reversal of conviction for armed robbery.

FACT SUMMARY: Crews (D) contended that since his first arrest was made without probable cause, his subsequent identification should have been suppressed.

CONCISE RULE OF LAW: A witness' in-court identification of the defendant may not be excluded as being the fruit of an illegal detention of the defendant.

FACTS: Three women were robbed at gunpoint in the women's restroom on the grounds of the Washington Monument. Crews (D), who matched the general description given, was taken into custody because he was a truant. Before he was released, Crews (D) was questioned and photographed. The following day, one of the victims was looking through photographs when she picked out the picture of Crews (D). One of the other victims made a similar identification. Crews (D) was taken into custody, and at a court-ordered lineup, he was positively identified by the two women. Crews (D) filed a pre-trial motion to suppress all identification testimony. The court ruled that because Crews' (D) first arrest lacked probable cause, the products of the arrest — the photographic and lineup identifications — could not be introduced at trial. But, the judge allowed an in-court identification, and Crews (D) was convicted of armed robbery of one of the victims. The District of Columbia Court of Appeals reversed Crews' (D) conviction and ordered the suppression of the first robbery victim's in-court identification. The Government (P) appealed.

ISSUE: May a witness' in-court identification of the defendant be excluded as being the fruit of an illegal detention of the defendant?

HOLDING AND DECISION: (Brennan, J.) No. A witness' in-court identification of the defendant may not be excluded as being the fruit of an illegal detention of the defendant. A victim's in-court identification has three distinct elements. First, the victim is present at trial to testify as to what transpired between her and the offender, and to identify the defendant as the culprit. Second, the victim possesses knowledge of and the ability to reconstruct the prior criminal occurrence and to identify the defendant from her observations of him at the time of the crime. And third, the defendant is also physically present in the courtroom so the victim can observe him and compare his appearance to that of the offender. None of these three elements has been come at by exploitation of the violation of Crews' (D) Fourth Amendment rights. Reversed.

CONCURRENCE: (White, J.) The evidence ordered suppressed was eyewitness testimony of the victim which was not the product of Crews' (D) arrest. The fact that Crews (D) was present at trial and therefore capable of being identified by the victim is merely the inevitable result of the trial being held, which is permissible under Frisbie v. Collins, 342 U.S. 519 (1952).

EDITOR'S ANALYSIS: Justice Brennan also appears to adopt the inevitable discovery doctrine in part of his analysis. Inevitable discovery, which is evidence that would otherwise be regarded as the inadmissible fruit of the poisonous tree, may nonetheless be admitted if the evidence probably or "inevitably" would have been discovered without regard to the illegality.

[For more information on fruit of the poisonous tree, see Casenote Law Outline on Criminal Procedure, Chapter 15, § V, "Fruit of the Poisonous Tree" Doctrine.]

NOTES:

UNITED STATES v. LEON
468 U.S. 897 (1984).

NATURE OF CASE: Appeal from grant of motion to suppress in prosecution for narcotics.

FACT SUMMARY: The Government (P) contended that evidence obtained from a defective search warrant should not be excluded because the police relied in good faith on that warrant.

CONCISE RULE OF LAW: Evidence will not be excluded where police rely in good faith on a defective search warrant.

FACTS: Police officers received a tip from an informant of unproven reliability that two of the defendants were selling narcotics. An experienced narcotics investigator prepared an application for a search warrant and an affidavit that related information from the tip and the investigation. The application was reviewed, and a facially valid warrant was issued. The subsequent search revealed narcotics, and Leon (D) and the other defendants were indicted for various drug offenses. The district court granted Leon's (D) motion to suppress because the affidavit was insufficient to establish probable cause. However, the court made clear that the investigator had acted in good faith. The court of appeals affirmed. The Government (P) appealed solely on the question of whether the exclusionary rule should be modified so as not to bar the admission of evidence seized in reasonable, good-faith reliance on a search warrant that is subsequently held to be defective.

ISSUE: Should evidence be excluded where police rely in good faith on a defective search warrant?

HOLDING AND DECISION: (White, J.) No. Evidence will not be excluded where police rely in good faith on a defective search warrant. The marginal or nonexistent benefits produced by suppressing evidence obtained in objectively reasonable reliance on a subsequently invalidated search warrant cannot justify the substantial costs of exclusion. The investigator's application for a warrant clearly was supported by much more than a "bare bones" affidavit. The affidavit related the results of an extensive investigation and, as the divided panel of the court of appeals made clear, provided evidence sufficient to create disagreement among thoughtful and competent judges as to the existence of probable cause. Under these circumstances, the officers' reliance on the magistrate's determination of probable cause was objectively reasonable, and, thus, exclusion was inappropriate. Reversed.

DISSENT: (Brennan, J.) The full impact of the Court's regrettable decision will not be felt until the Court attempts to extend this rule to situations in which the police have conducted a warrantless search solely on the basis of their own judgment about the existence of probable cause and exigent circumstances. When that question is finally posed, it would not be surprising if the other justices decide once again that we simply can't afford to protect Fourth Amendment rights.

EDITOR'S ANALYSIS: One of the keys to the majority's conclusion is its belief that the prospective deterrent effect of the exclusionary rule operates only in those situations in which police officers, when deciding whether to go forward with some particular search, have reason to know that their planned conduct will violate the requirements of the Fourth Amendment. When police officers act in good faith on a warrant, no such deterrent effect of the exclusionary rule exists.

[For more information on the good-faith exception to the exclusionary rule, see Casenote Law Outline on Criminal Procedure, Chapter 5, § IV, "Particularity."]

NOTES:

NOTES

CHAPTER 8
ENTRAPMENT, DUE PROCESS, AND THE SUPERVISORY POWER - ALTERNATIVES TO THE FOURTH AMENDMENT FOR REGULATING POLICE UNDERCOVER ACTIVITIES

QUICK REFERENCE RULES OF LAW

1. **Entrapment.** Where government actions create a person's disposition to commit a crime, and then the government suggests the crime which that person commits, it is entrapment. (Jacobson v. United States)

   [For more information on entrapment, see Casenote Law Outline on Criminal Procedure, Chapter 16, §§ I -IV.]

2. **Supervisory Power of the Federal Courts.** The supervisory power of the federal courts does not include authorization to suppress otherwise admissible evidence on the ground that it was seized unlawfully from a third party not before the court. (United States v. Payner)

   [For more information on the supervisory power of federal courts, see Casenote Law Outline on Criminal Procedure, Chapter 15, § II, The Policy Debate.]

NOTES

JACOBSON v. UNITED STATES
112 S. Ct. 1535 (1992).

NATURE OF CASE: Appeal of conviction for receiving child pornography.

FACT SUMMARY: Jacobson (D) claimed the Government (P) had entrapped him into violating a child pornography law.

CONCISE RULE OF LAW: Where government actions create a person's disposition to commit a crime, and then the government suggests the crime which that person commits, it is entrapment.

FACTS: At a time when it was legal, Jacobson (D) ordered from an adult bookstore two magazines picturing nude boys, though he later testified he thought he was ordering photos of young men over 17. Congress subsequently passed the Child Protection Act of 1984, criminalizing receipt by mail of sexually explicit depictions of children. The Postal Service found Jacobson's (D) name on the store's mailing list and began mailing Jacobson (D) letters and questionnaires from fictitious research and lobbying organizations and a fake pen pal. The mailings discussed and asked about Jacobson's (D) tastes in pornography and views on censorship. Each time he answered, the next mailing was fit more to his tastes. After two years, the Customs Service, through a fake company, sent Jacobson (D) a child pornography brochure. He placed an order, but it was never filled. The Postal Service, using a fake company, sent Jacobson (D) a letter decrying censorship and claiming the media and government were trying to keep its material out of the country. Jacobson (D) requested a catalogue, from which he later ordered child pornography. Jacobson (D) was arrested upon controlled delivery of the magazine. He unsuccessfully raised an entrapment defense and was convicted under the 1984 Act. The court of appeals affirmed, and Jacobson (D) appealed.

ISSUE: Where government actions create a person's disposition to commit a crime, and then the government suggests the crime which that person consents, is it entrapment?

HOLDING AND DECISION: (White, J.) Yes. Where government acts create a person's disposition to commit a crime, and then the government suggests the crime which that person commits, it is entrapment. Jacobson (D) had become predisposed to break the law by the time he ordered a magazine from the Government (P). However, the Government (P) did not prove this disposition was not the product of years of Government (P) targeting. The magazines Jacobson (D) ordered from the bookstore were legal when bought. Evidence of predisposition to do what was once legal is not sufficient to show predisposition to do what now is illegal, since most people obey laws they disagree with. Jacobson's (D) claim that he did not know he was ordering photos of minors from the bookstore was unchallenged. His answers to Government (P) mailings showed predisposition to view child pornography and to support a given agenda through lobbying groups but did not support an inference of predisposition to commit the alleged crime. The strong arguable inference is that by waving the banner of individual rights and disparaging efforts to restrict pornography, the Government (P) excited Jacobson's (D) interest in banned materials and exerted substantial pressure on him to fight censorship by obtaining such materials. The government may not play on an innocent man's weaknesses and beguile him into committing crimes he would not commit otherwise. Reversed.

DISSENT: (O'Connor, J.) Both times the Government (P) offered Jacobson (D) a chance to buy pornography he responded enthusiastically. Thus, a reasonable jury could find a predisposition to commit the crime. Predisposition should be assessed as of the time the government suggested the crime, not when the government first became involved; the government does not need a reasonable suspicion before it can investigate. Moreover, the two-year investigation of Jacobson (D) involved no threats, coercion, or "substantial pressure" to commit the crime. Finally, the Government (P) did not have to prove Jacobson (D) was predisposed to break the law, only that he was predisposed to receive child pornography. The 1984 Act does not require specific intent to break the law, only knowing receipt. Since the requirement of predisposition is designed to eliminate the entrapment defense for those who would have committed the crime absent government inducement, the elements of predisposition should track the elements of the crime.

EDITOR'S ANALYSIS: The Court follows the subjective test for entrapment, i.e., whether the defendant was predisposed to commit the crime, as opposed to the objective test, i.e., whether police conduct created a substantial risk that an innocent person would commit the crime. However, as the dissent points out, the Court's main concern "is that the Government went too far and 'abused' the 'processes of detection and enforcement' by luring an innocent person to violate the law." Jacobson illustrates how the subjective and objective tests are blurred in application. In analyzing an entrapment claim, courts must look to the conduct of both the defendant and the police.

[For more information on entrapment, see Casenote Law Outline on Criminal Procedure, Chapter 16, §§ I - IV.]

NOTES:

UNITED STATES v. PAYNER
447 U.S. 727 (1980).

NATURE OF CASE: Appeal from grant of motion to suppress in prosecution for falsification of federal income tax return.

FACT SUMMARY: Payner (D) contended that his bank account information should be suppressed because it was obtained from an illegal search.

CONCISE RULE OF LAW: The supervisory power of the federal courts does not include authorization to suppress otherwise admissible evidence on the ground that it was seized unlawfully from a third party not before the court.

FACTS: Payner (D) was indicted for falsifying his 1972 federal income tax return. The indictment alleged that Payner (D) denied maintaining a foreign bank account when he knew that he had such an account at the Castle Bank of Nassau. The Government's (P) case rested heavily on a loan guarantee agreement which the Government (P) discovered by exploiting an illegal search. IRS suspicion focused on Castle Bank in 1972, when investigators learned that a suspected narcotics trafficker had an account there. An IRS agent conspired with a private investigator, who illegally obtained bank records a Castle Bank vice president had in his possession. The documents showed a close working relationship between Castle Bank and a Florida bank. Subpoenas issued to the Florida bank uncovered the loan guarantee agreement at issue in this case. The district court suppressed the evidence, and as a result, there was insufficient evidence to sustain a conviction. The court of appeals affirmed, and the Government (P) appealed.

ISSUE: Does the supervisory power of the federal courts include authorization to suppress otherwise admissible evidence on the ground that it was seized unlawfully from a third party not before the court?

HOLDING AND DECISION: (Powell, J.) No. The supervisory power of the federal courts does not include authorization to suppress otherwise admissible evidence on the ground that it was seized unlawfully from a third party not before the court. The Court's Fourth Amendment decisions have established beyond any doubt that the interest in deterring illegal searches does not justify the exclusion of tainted evidence at the instance of a party who was not the victim of the challenged practices. The lower court's reasoning amounts to a substitution of individual judgment for the controlling decisions of this Court. Were this Court to accept this use of the supervisory power, it would confer on the judiciary discretionary power to disregard the considered limitations of the law it is charged with enforcing. The supervisory power does not extend so far. Reversed.

EDITOR'S ANALYSIS: Federal courts may use their supervisory power in some circumstances to exclude evidence taken from the defendant by "willful disobedience of law." McNabb v. United States, 318 U.S. 332 (1943). The Supreme Court has never held, however, that the supervisory power authorizes suppression of evidence obtained from third parties in violation of the Constitution, a statute, or a rule. The supervisory power merely permits federal courts to supervise "the administration of criminal justice" among the parties before the bar.

[For more information on the supervisory power of federal courts, see Casenote Law Outline on Criminal Procedure, Chapter 15, § II, The Policy Debate.]

NOTES:

CHAPTER 9
THE FIFTH AMENDMENT

QUICK REFERENCE RULES

1. **The Justifications for the Fifth Amendment Privilege against Self-incrimination.** If a witness' testimony will not incriminate him because he has secured legal immunity from prosecution, the witness is not entitled to the privilege of silence. (Brown v. Walker)

2. **The Justifications for the Fifth Amendment Privilege against Self-incrimination.** The sole concern of the Fifth Amendment privilege is the danger to a witness forced to give testimony leading to the infliction of penalties affixed to criminal acts. (Ullman v. United States)

3. **The Justifications for the Fifth Amendment Privilege against Self-incrimination.** Testimony may be compelled if immunity from prosecution is granted; no Fifth Amendment violation occurs. (Kastigar v. United States)

4. **Testimony.** A court order compelling a target of a grand jury investigation to authorize foreign banks to disclose records of his accounts without identifying those documents or acknowledging their existence does not violate the target's Fifth Amendment privilege against self-incrimination. (Doe v. United States)

5. **Changing Social Conditions and Self-incrimination.** The requirement that motorists involved in accidents leave their names at the scene of an accident does not entail a substantial risk of self-incrimination. (California v. Byers)

6. **Changing Social Conditions and Self-incrimination.** The Fifth Amendment does not prevent the government from introducing into evidence an alleged drunk driver's refusal to submit to a blood-alcohol test even though he was not warned that his refusal might be used against him. (South Dakota v. Neville)

7. **Child Custody and Self-incrimination.** A parent, who is the custodian of a child pursuant to a court order, may not invoke the Fifth Amendment privilege against self-incrimination to resist an order of the juvenile court to produce the child. (Baltimore Department of Social Service v. Bouknight)

8. **Coerced Confessions.** In the context of the Fifth Amendment privilege against self-incrimination, a confession will be suppressed if any degree of influence is exerted by the police. (Bram v. United States)

   [For more information on coerced confessions, see Casenote Law Outline on Criminal Procedure, Chapter 18, § II, Voluntariness versus Coercion.]

9. **Sixth Amendment Interrogation Rights.** After the accused has been indicted, the Sixth Amendment forbids the use at trial of incriminating statements deliberately elicited from the accused by government agents in the absence of counsel. (Massiah v. United States)

   [For more information on Sixth Amendment interrogation rights, see Casenote Law Outline on Criminal Procedure, Chapter 20, § I, The Massiah Right-to-Counsel Doctrine.]

10. **Miranda Rights.** A defendant's statement may not be offered into evidence if it results from custodial interrogation of the defendant by the government unless warnings under the Fifth Amendment have been given to the defendant. (Miranda v. Arizona)

    [For more information on Miranda rights, see Casenote Law Outline on Criminal Procedure, Chapter 19, §§ I-IX.]

11. **Interrogation.** There is no interrogation where comments by one officer to another officer about the dangerousness of the crime elicit a response from the suspect. (Rhode Island v. Innis)

[For more information on interrogation, see Casenote Law Outline on Criminal Procedure, Chapter 19, § VI, "Interrogation."]

12. **"Testimonial."** In order to be testimonial, an accused's communication must, itself, explicitly or implicitly relate a factual assertion or disclose information. (Pennsylvania v. Muniz)

13. **Interrogation.** A statement made by a probationer to his probation officer without prior warnings of his privilege against self-incrimination is admissible in a subsequent criminal proceeding. (Minnesota v. Murphy)

   [For more information on interrogation, see Casenote Law Outline on Criminal Procedure, Chapter 19, § I, Miranda in Historical Context.]

14. **Police Interrogation.** Miranda warnings are not required when the suspect is unaware that he is speaking to a law enforcement officer and gives a voluntary statement. (Illinois v. Perkins)

   [For more information on police interrogation, see Casenote Law Outline on Criminal Procedure, Chapter 19, § VI, "Interrogation."]

15. **Waiver.** A prearraignment confession preceded by an otherwise valid waiver is not tainted by unrelated police misconduct. (Moran v. Burbine)

16. **Waiver.** An accused waives his previously invoked right to counsel when he reopens dialogue about the subject matter of the criminal investigation. (Oregon v. Bradshaw)

17. **Custodial Interrogation.** Ambiguous statements made during custodial interrogation regarding the desire for an attorney may not preclude further interrogation. (Davis v. United States)

   [For more information on custodial interrogation, see Casenote Law Outline on Criminal Procedure, Chapter 19, § VIII.]

18. **Adversary Judicial Proceedings.** Once adversary proceedings have commenced against an individual, he has a right to legal representation when the government interrogates him. (Brewer v. Williams)

   [For more information on adversary judicial proceedings, see Casenote Law Outline on Criminal Procedure, Chapter 20, § II, "Adversary Judicial Criminal Proceedings".]

19. **Waiver of the Right to Counsel.** Police may not initiate any interrogation after a defendant asserts his right to counsel at an arraignment or similar proceeding without a valid waiver of the defendant's right to counsel. (Michigan v. Jackson)

   [For more information on waiver of the right to counsel, see Casenote Law Outline on Criminal Procedure, Chapter 20, § IV, Waiver of the Right to Counsel.]

20. **Sixth Amendment Right to Counsel.** An accused's invocation of his Sixth Amendment right to counsel during a judicial proceeding does not constitute an invocation of his Miranda right to counsel. (McNeil v. Wisconsin)

   [For more information on the Sixth Amendment right to counsel, see Casenote Law Outline on Criminal Procedure, Chapter 20, § I, The Massiah Right-to-Counsel Doctrine.]

21. **Exceptions to the Miranda Rule.** Statements made by a suspect before Miranda warnings are given are admissible under a "public safety" exception if elicited by police because of a genuine need to protect the public. (New York v. Quarles)

[For more information on exceptions to the Miranda rule, see Casenote Law Outline on Criminal Procedure, Chapter 19, § VII, Exceptions to the Miranda Rule.]

22. **The Miranda Exclusionary Rule.** A voluntary confession given after Miranda warnings are administered is not tainted by a first confession given prior to such warnings. (Oregon v. Elstad)

    [For more information on the Miranda Exclusionary Rule, see Casenote Law Outline on Criminal Procedure, Chapter 19, § IX, Miranda Exclusionary Rule.]

23. **"Voluntariness."** Absent governmental coercion, the Fifth Amendment privilege is not concerned with moral and psychological pressures to confess emanating from sources other than official coercion. (Colorado v. Connelly)

NOTES

BROWN v. WALKER
161 U.S. 591 (1896).

NATURE OF CASE: Appeal from a denial of invoking the Fifth Amendment privilege against self-incrimination.

FACT SUMMARY: Brown (D) contended that he had the right to refuse to answer questions put forth to him by the grand jury because his answers might incriminate him.

CONCISE RULE OF LAW: If a witness' testimony will not incriminate him because he has secured legal immunity from prosecution, the witness is not entitled to the privilege of silence.

FACTS: The grand jury was engaged in investigating certain alleged violations of the Interstate Commerce Act by the Allegheny Valley Railway Company, for which Brown (D) was the auditor. Brown (D) was asked whether he knew of any discrimination in favor of the Union Coal Company by Allegheny. He declined to answer because he might incriminate himself. It was clear that Brown (D) was not an offender against the law, and his privilege was claimed for the purpose of shielding Allegheny from criminal charges. Brown's (D) refusal to answer violated a congressional act, which stated that no person shall be excused from testifying before the Interstate Commerce Commission on self-incrimination grounds, although no person shall be prosecuted or subjected to any penalty or forfeiture concerning which he may testify to. Brown (D) appealed the ruling of the lower court, which held him in violation of the congressional act.

ISSUE: If a witness' testimony will not incriminate him because he has secured legal immunity from prosecution, should that witness be entitled to invoke the privilege of silence?

HOLDING AND DECISION: (Brown, J.) No. If a witness' testimony will not incriminate him because he has secured legal immunity from prosecution, the witness is not entitled to the privilege of silence. The design of the constitutional privilege is not to aid the witness in vindicating his character but to protect him against being compelled to furnish evidence to convict him of a criminal charge. If he secures legal immunity from prosecution, the possible impairment of his good name is a penalty which he should be compelled to pay for the common good. While the constitutional provision in question is justly regarded as one of the most valuable prerogatives of the citizen, the object is fully accomplished by the statutory immunity, and, therefore, Brown (D) was properly compelled to answer. Affirmed.

DISSENT: (Shiras, J.) The effect of the congressional act in question, as a protection to the witness, is purely conjectural. No court can foresee all the results and consequences that may follow from enforcing this law in any given case. It is quite certain that if a witness is compelled to testify against himself, and if he can't procure the evidence that will be necessary to maintain his plea, he will be subjected to the hazard of a charge of perjury.

EDITOR'S ANALYSIS: The danger of extending the principle announced in Counselman v. Hitchcock, 142 U.S. 547 (1892), is that the privilege may be put forward for a sentimental reason or for a purely fanciful protection of the witness against an imaginary danger, and for the real purpose of securing immunity to some third person who is interested in concealing the facts to which he would testify. No citizen has the right to permit himself, under the pretext of shielding his own good name, to be made the tool of others who are desirous of seeking shelter behind the privilege.

NOTES:

ULLMANN v. UNITED STATES
350 U.S. 422 (1956).

NATURE OF CASE: Appeal from a denial of invoking the Fifth Amendment privilege against self-incrimination.

FACT SUMMARY: Ullmann (D) contended that he should be able to invoke the Fifth Amendment privilege at a grand jury hearing because the impact of the disabilities imposed by federal and state authorities and the public would be so oppressive that he would not have true immunity.

CONCISE RULE OF LAW: The sole concern of the Fifth Amendment privilege is the danger to a witness forced to give testimony leading to the infliction of penalties affixed to criminal acts.

FACTS: Ullmann (D) was asked during a grand jury hearing whether or not he was a Communist. Ullmann (D) chose not to answer the question and invoked the Fifth Amendment privilege. Even though Ullmann (D) was free from prosecution, he chose to invoke the privilege because he could be subjected to expulsion from labor unions, loss of job and passport eligibility, and general public scorn. However, the lower court held that since he was protected under the Immunity Act, and thus free from prosecution, Ullmann (D) was compelled to answer. The court of appeals affirmed, and Ullmann (D) appealed.

ISSUE: Is the sole concern of the Fifth Amendment privilege the danger to a witness forced to give testimony leading to the infliction of penalties affixed to criminal acts?

HOLDING AND DECISION: (Frankfurter, J.) Yes. The sole concern of the Fifth Amendment privilege is the danger to a witness forced to give testimony leading to the infliction of penalties affixed to criminal acts. This Court has often held that the immunity granted need only remove those sanctions which generate the fear justifying invocation of the privilege. Immunity displaces the danger. Once the reason for the privilege ceases, the privilege ceases. Affirmed.

DISSENT: (Douglas, J.) There is no indication that the Immunity Act grants protection against the disabilities Ullmann (D) claimed he would suffer. This Court in Counselman v. Hitchcock, 142 U.S. 547 (1892), held that for an immunity statute to be valid, it must "supply a complete protection from all of the perils against which the constitutional prohibition was designed to guard." At stake if Ullmann (D) was compelled to testify was the possible forfeiture of his citizenship rights. Any forfeiture of rights as a result of compelled testimony is at war with the Fifth Amendment. When public opinion casts a person into the outer darkness, as happens (during the time when this case was decided) when a person is exposed as a Communist, the government brings infamy on the head of the witness when it compels disclosure. That is precisely what the Fifth Amendment prohibits.

EDITOR'S ANALYSIS: Justice Douglas' dissent relies heavily on Boyd v. United States, 116 U.S. 616 (1886), where the Court held that forfeiture of property as the result of compelled testimony was a valid reason to invoke the privilege. Yet, in the case at hand, the majority chose only to look at whether or not testimony may expose the witness to a criminal charge. The majority cited Hale v. Henkel, 201 U.S. 43, in pointing out that if the criminality has already been taken away, the privilege ceases to apply.

NOTES:

KASTIGAR v. UNITED STATES
406 U.S. 441 (1972).

NATURE OF CASE: Action to quash contempt citation.

FACT SUMMARY: After being given prosecutorial immunity, Kastigar (D) still refused to testify before a grand jury on Fifth Amendment grounds.

CONCISE RULE OF LAW: Testimony may be compelled if immunity from prosecution is granted; no Fifth Amendment violation occurs.

FACTS: Kastigar (D) was subpoenaed to testify before a grand jury. The U.S. attorney obtained prosecutorial immunity for Kastigar (D) since he felt that the Fifth Amendment would be invoked. Kastigar (D) refused to testify anyway invoking the Fifth Amendment. Kastigar (D) was cited for contempt and imprisoned. Kastigar (D) appealed alleging that prosecutorial immunity was not coextensive with Fifth Amendment rights.

ISSUE: Is the protection afforded by prosecutorial immunity coextensive with the protection of the Fifth Amendment so that a party may be compelled to testify?

HOLDING AND DECISION: (Powell, J.) Yes. First, prosecutorial immunity from any statements made before the grand jury prevents the prosecution for anything but perjury. Therefore there is no self-incrimination with respect to any present or future criminal proceedings and the privilege is inapplicable. Where the privilege cannot be raised the state may compel testimony in grand jury hearings. If the protection offered by prosecutorial immunity is coextensive with that of the Fifth Amendment the contempt citation must stand. Kastigar (D) alleged that full transactional immunity must be granted to be coextensive with the privilege against self-incrimination. Prosecutorial immunity merely grants immunity for the subject of the testimony or its fruits. No absolute immunity is granted for future prosecutions. The proscription of the use of the testimony or evidence in any future criminal prosecution is coextensive with Fifth Amendment protection. The immunity bars the use of the information for any leads. The contempt citation is affirmed.

DISSENT: (Douglas, J.) When this Court allows the prosecution to offer only "use" immunity, far less is granted than taken away. For while the precise testimony that it is compelled may not be used, leads from that testimony may be pursued and used to convict the witness. The Self-Incrimination Clause creates "the federally protected right of silence," making it unconstitutional to use a law "to pry open one's lips and make him a witness against himself." That is one of the chief procedural guarantees in our accusatorial system. Therefore, this Court must adhere to Counselman v. Hitchcock, 142 U.S. 547 (1892), and hold that this attempt to dilute the Self-Incrimination Clause is unconstitutional.

DISSENT: (Marshall, J.) Use immunity does not prevent future prosecution for crimes admitted during the compelled testimony. All the prosecution must do to bring a subsequent action is show that the information was obtained from independent sources. Merely placing a heavy burden on the prosecution does not adequately protect the defendant. There is too great a possibility for abuse.

EDITOR'S ANALYSIS: In the companion case, Zicarelli v. New Jersey State Commission of Investigation, 406 U.S. 472 (1972), the Court upheld a similar state use statute. There was also upheld a requirement of responsive answers. Immunity would not be enlarged by unresponsive answers which tended to enlarge the scope of the immunity by including other wrongdoing. A state may grant immunity and the testimony cannot be used in another state or in a federal prosecution. Murphy v. Waterfront Common, 378 U.S. 52 (1964).

NOTES:

DOE v. UNITED STATES
487 U.S. 201 (1988).

NATURE OF CASE: Appeal from an order compelling the authorization of bank records.

FACT SUMMARY: Doe (D) contended that compelling him to authorize foreign banks to disclose records of his accounts violated his Fifth Amendment privilege against self-incrimination.

CONCISE RULE OF LAW: A court order compelling a target of a grand jury investigation to authorize foreign banks to disclose records of his accounts without identifying those documents or acknowledging their existence does not violate the target's Fifth Amendment privilege against self-incrimination.

FACTS: Doe (D) was the target of a grand jury investigation into possible federal offenses. A subpoena directed him to produce records from three named banks in the Cayman Islands and Bermuda. Doe (D) produced some records and testified that there were no others. When questioned about the existence of additional records, Doe (D) invoked his Fifth Amendment privilege. The U.S. branches of three foreign banks also were served with subpoenas ordering them to produce records of accounts over which Doe (D) had signatory authority. Citing their secrecy laws, the banks refused to comply without Doe's (D) consent. The Government (P) then moved that the court order Doe (D) to sign 12 forms consenting to disclosure of any bank records relating to 12 foreign bank accounts of which he had control. The district court denied the motion because compelling Doe (D) to sign the forms was prohibited by the Fifth Amendment. The Government (P) sought reconsideration after a revised proposal, but that motion was also denied. The court of appeals reversed, and Doe (D) appealed.

ISSUE: Does a court order compelling a target of a grand jury investigation to authorize foreign banks to disclose records of his accounts without identifying those documents or acknowledging their existence violate the target's Fifth Amendment privilege against self-incrimination?

HOLDING AND DECISION: (Blackmun, J.) No. A court order compelling a target of a grand jury investigation to authorize foreign banks to disclose records of his accounts without identifying those documents or acknowledging their existence does not violate the target's Fifth Amendment privilege against self-incrimination. The question on which this case turns is whether the act of executing the form is a "testimonial communication." The consent directive itself is not "testimonial." It is carefully drafted not to make reference to a specific account but only to speak in the hypothetical. By signing the form, Doe (D) makes no statement regarding the existence of a foreign bank account. In addition, in its testimonial significance, the execution of such a directive is analogous to the production of a handwriting sample or voice exemplar; it is a nontestimonial act and, therefore, not violative of the Fifth Amendment privilege against self-incrimination. Affirmed.

DISSENT: (Stevens, J.) If Doe (D) can be compelled to use his mind to assist the Government (P) in developing its case, he will be forced to be a witness against himself.

EDITOR'S ANALYSIS: It should be noted that the contents of the foreign bank records sought by the Government (P) were not privileged under the Fifth Amendment. In addition, there is also no question that the foreign banks cannot invoke the Fifth Amendment to decline to produce the documents; the privilege does not extend to such artificial entities.

NOTES:

CALIFORNIA v. BYERS
402 U.S. 424 (1971).

NATURE OF CASE: Appeal from demurrer to prosecution for vehicle code violations.

FACT SUMMARY: Byers (D) contended that a California statute requiring him to stop and identify himself after being involved in an accident violated his Fifth Amendment privilege against self-incrimination.

CONCISE RULE OF LAW: The requirement that motorists involved in accidents leave their names at the scene of an accident does not entail a substantial risk of self-incrimination.

FACTS: Byers (D) was charged in a two-count criminal complaint with two misdemeanor violations of the California Vehicle Code. The count at issue charged Byers (D) with failing to stop and identify himself after being involved in an accident, as required by § 2002(a)(1). Byers (D) demurred to the court on the ground that it violated his privilege against compulsory self-incrimination. His position was ultimately sustained by the California Supreme Court. That court held that the privilege protected a driver who "reasonably believes that compliance with the statute will result in self-incrimination." The court found that Byers' (D) apprehensions were reasonable. Nevertheless, the court upheld the validity of the statute by inserting a judicially created use restriction but did not punish Byers (D) because he could not have reasonably anticipated the judicial promulgation of the restriction. The U.S. Supreme Court granted certiorari to determine whether the California statute without the use restriction violated the privilege against compulsory self-incrimination.

ISSUE: Does requiring motorists involved in accidents to leave their names at the scene of an accident entail a substantial risk of self-incrimination?

HOLDING AND DECISION: (Burger, C.J.) No. The requirement that motorists involved in accidents leave their names at the scene of an accident does not entail a substantial risk of self-incrimination. Although identity, when made known, may lead to inquiry that in turn leads to arrest and charge, those developments depend on different factors and independent evidence. Here, the compelled disclosure of identity could have led to a charge that might not have been made had the driver fled the scene, but this is true only in the same sense that a taxpayer can be charged on the basis of the contents of a tax return or failure to file an income tax form. There is no constitutional right to refuse to file an income tax return or to flee the scene of an accident in order to avoid the possibility of legal involvement. Vacated and remanded.

CONCURRENCE: (Harlan, J.) California's decision to compel Byers (D) to stop after his accident and identify himself will not relieve the state of the duty to determine by its own investigation whether or not Byers' (D) behavior was criminal. In short, once one has focused attention on himself as an accident participant, the state must still bear the burden of making the main evidentiary case against him.

DISSENT: (Brennan, J.) One of the primary flaws of the plurality opinion is that it bears so little relationship to the case at hand. Notwithstanding the fact that Byers (D) was charged both with a violation which resulted in an accident and with failing to report the accident as required by the statute under review, the plurality concludes, contrary to all three California courts below, that Byers (D) was faced with no substantial hazard of self-incrimination under California law. In Marchetti v. United States, 390 U.S. 39 (1968), and Albertson v. Subversive Activities Control Board, 382 U.S. 70 (1965), the facts were not necessarily criminal, and this Court had to determine whether the petitioners faced "real and appreciable" or merely "imaginary and unsubstantial" hazards when they refused to register. By contrast, in the present case, it is hard to imagine a record demonstrating a more substantial hazard of self-incrimination than this.

EDITOR'S ANALYSIS: Justice Black's dissent points to how the plurality's opinion sought to distinguish this case from previous decisions on the ground that the California statute required disclosure in an area not "permeated with criminal statutes" and because it was not aimed at a "highly selective group inherently suspect of criminal activities." However, those suggestions ignored the fact that Byers (D), in this case, would have run a serious risk of self-incrimination by complying with the disclosure statute.

NOTES:

SOUTH DAKOTA v. NEVILLE
459 U.S. 553 (1983).

NATURE OF CASE: Appeal from grant of motion to suppress in prosecution for drunk driving.

FACT SUMMARY: Neville (D) contended that a South Dakota (P) law allowing the introduction into evidence of his refusal to take a blood-alcohol test violated his Fifth Amendment privilege against self-incrimination.

CONCISE RULE OF LAW: The Fifth Amendment does not prevent the government from introducing into evidence an alleged drunk driver's refusal to submit to a blood-alcohol test even though he was not warned that his refusal might be used against him.

FACTS: Neville (D) was stopped by the police after he failed to stop at a stop sign. The officers asked Neville (D) for his license and to get out of the car. As he exited his car, Neville (D) staggered and fell against his car. The officers smelled alcohol on his breath and asked him to perform field sobriety tests. When Neville (D) failed the tests, he was arrested and read his rights. Neville (D) stated he understood his rights and agreed to talk. The officers asked Neville (D) to submit to a blood-alcohol test and warned him that he could lose his license if he refused. Neville (D) refused, stating that he was too drunk and wouldn't pass the test. Subsequently, Neville (D) refused to take the test again down at the police station. Even though South Dakota (P) law allows evidence of a refusal to submit to a blood-alcohol test at trial, Neville (D) still moved to suppress the evidence. The circuit court granted the suppression motion. The South Dakota Supreme Court affirmed, stating that the law violated the federal and state privilege against self-incrimination.

ISSUE: Does the Fifth Amendment prevent the government from introducing into evidence an alleged drunk driver's refusal to submit to a blood-alcohol test even though he was not warned that his refusal might be used against him?

HOLDING AND DECISION: (O'Connor, J.) No. The Fifth Amendment does not prevent the government from introducing into evidence an alleged drunk driver's refusal to submit to a blood-alcohol test even though he was not warned that his refusal might be used against him. The choice to submit or refuse to take a blood-alcohol test will not be an easy or pleasant one for a suspect to make. But the criminal process often requires suspects and defendants to make difficult choices. Therefore, a refusal to take a blood-alcohol test, after a police officer has lawfully requested it, is not an act coerced by the officer and, thus, is not protected by the privilege against self-incrimination. Reversed.

EDITOR'S ANALYSIS: This case stems from the landmark case of Schmerber v. California, 384 U.S. 757 (1966), which held that a state could force a defendant to submit to a blood-alcohol test without violating the defendant's Fifth Amendment rights. However, South Dakota has declined to authorize its police officers to administer a blood-alcohol test against the suspect's will. Instead, a refusal probably will lead to a driver's license being revoked for one year.

NOTES:

BALTIMORE CITY DEPARTMENT OF SOCIAL SERVICES v. BOUKNIGHT
110 S. Ct. 900 (1990).

NATURE OF CASE: Appeal from reversal of a contempt order.

FACT SUMMARY: Bouknight (D) contended that the contempt order issued by the juvenile court for her to produce her child violated her Fifth Amendment privilege against self-incrimination.

CONCISE RULE OF LAW: A parent, who is the custodian of a child pursuant to a court order, may not invoke the Fifth Amendment privilege against self-incrimination to resist an order of the juvenile court to produce the child.

FACTS: Bouknight (D) was under suspicion for abusing her child, Maurice. Baltimore Social Services (P) obtained a court order removing Maurice from Bouknight's (D) care. Shortly thereafter, Bouknight (D) regained custody of Maurice but under the continuing oversight of Baltimore Social Services (P). Eight months later, fearing for Maurice's safety, Baltimore Social Services (P) returned to juvenile court, stating that Bouknight (D) did not cooperate with them, violated the terms of the protective order, and could not provide adequate care for her child in general. The court then granted the petition to remove Maurice from Bouknight's (D) control for placement in foster care. Bouknight (D), however, failed to produce her child or say where he was. The court, fearing for Maurice's safety, issued a bench warrant for Bouknight's (D) appearance. After refusing again to produce her child, Bouknight (D) was found in contempt of court and ordered jailed until she produced the child. The juvenile court rejected Bouknight's (D) claim that the contempt order violated her Fifth Amendment rights. The court of appeals reversed, and this appeal followed.

ISSUE: May a parent, who is the custodian of a child pursuant to a court order, invoke the Fifth Amendment privilege against self-incrimination to resist an order of the juvenile court to produce the child?

HOLDING AND DECISION: (O'Connor, J.) No. A parent, who is the custodian of a child pursuant to a court order, may not invoke the Fifth Amendment privilege against self-incrimination to resist an order of the juvenile court to produce the child. A person may not claim the Fifth Amendment's protection based upon the incrimination that may result from the contents or nature of the thing demanded. Bouknight (D), therefore, cannot claim the privilege based upon anything that the examination of Maurice might reveal; nor can she assert the privilege upon the theory that compliance would assert that the child produced is in fact Maurice (a fact that the state could readily establish). The possibility that a production order will compel testimonial assertions that may prove incriminating does not, in all contexts, justify invoking the privilege to resist production. Concern for Maurice's safety was the reason for the order to produce him. The government demand for production of the very public charge entrusted to a custodian was made for compelling reasons unrelated to criminal law enforcement and as part of a broadly applied regulatory regime. In these circumstances, Bouknight (D) could not invoke the privilege to resist the order to produce Maurice. Reversed.

DISSENT: (Marshall, J.) The fact that the state throws a wide net in seeking information does not mean that it can demand from the few persons whose Fifth Amendment rights are implicated that they participate in their own criminal prosecutions. Rather, when the state demands testimony from its citizens, it should do so with an explicit grant of immunity.

EDITOR'S ANALYSIS: Justice Marshall also proposed a different analysis from that of the majority. Justice Marshall believed that an individualized inquiry is preferable because it allows the privilege to turn on the concrete facts of a particular case, rather than on abstract characterizations concerning the nature of a regulatory scheme. However, for case-by-case analysis to work, some clear guidelines are needed so that consistent and predictable results will be achieved.

NOTES:

BRAM v. UNITED STATES
168 U.S. 532 (1897).

NATURE OF CASE: Appeal from conviction for murder.

FACT SUMMARY: Bram (D) contended that a conversation between a detective and himself was erroneously admitted as a confession because it was not shown to be voluntary.

CONCISE RULE OF LAW: In the context of the Fifth Amendment privilege against self-incrimination, a confession will be suppressed if any degree of influence is exerted by the police.

FACTS: Bram (D), the first officer of the ship he worked on, was accused of murdering Nash, the captain, Nash's wife, and the ship's second mate. The crime was committed on the high seas. Bram (D) and another man, Brown, both suspects, were in the custody of the Halifax police, in Canada, awaiting the arrival of the United States consul, who was to bring formal charges. Before the consul's arrival, a police detective had Bram (D) brought from jail to his private office, and while alone with the detective, Bram (D) was stripped of his clothing. The detective told Bram (D) that Brown made a statement that he saw Bram (D) commit the murder. Bram (D) answered that Brown could not have seen him and asked where Brown was. The detective gave an answer to which Bram (D) responded that Brown could not have seen him from there. These statements were used as a confession by Bram (D), and he was convicted of murder. Bram (D) appealed.

ISSUE: In the context of the Fifth Amendment privilege against self-incrimination, will a confession be suppressed if any degree of influence is exerted by the police?

HOLDING AND DECISION: (White, J.) Yes. In the context of the Fifth Amendment privilege against self-incrimination, a confession will be suppressed if any degree of influence is exerted by the police. A statement must not be extracted by any sorts of threat or violence nor obtained by any direct or implied promises, however slight, nor by the exertion of any improper influence. The situation of the accused, and the nature of the communication made to him by the detective, necessarily overthrows any possible implication that Bram's (D) reply to the detective could have been the result of a purely voluntary mental action. The statement made by the detective was aimed to produce upon Bram's (D) mind the fear that if he remained silent it would be considered an admission of guilt. Error was committed by the trial court in admitting the confession. Reversed.

EDITOR'S ANALYSIS: The Bram decision had little immediate impact for two reasons. First, it was not until 1964 that the Supreme Court ruled that the Fifth Amendment privilege was applicable to the states. Thus, the rule was limited to federal cases. Second, although Bram (D) invoked the Fifth Amendment, without dissent on this point, the standard actually employed was the voluntariness standard of the common law.

[For more information on coerced confessions, see Casenote Law Outline on Criminal Procedure, Chapter 18, § II, Voluntariness versus Coercion.]

NOTES:

MASSIAH v. UNITED STATES
377 U.S. 201 (1964).

NATURE OF CASE: Review of conviction for narcotics possession.

FACT SUMMARY: While free on bail following his indictment and arraignment, Massiah (D) made incriminating statements to an accomplice who had secretly agreed with authorities to act as an informer.

CONCISE RULE OF LAW: After the accused has been indicted, the Sixth Amendment forbids the use at trial of incriminating statements deliberately elicited from the accused by government agents in the absence of counsel.

FACTS: Massiah (D) was arrested, arraigned, and indicted for possession of narcotics. He retained a lawyer, pleaded not guilty, and was released on bail. In the same indictment naming Massiah (D), Colson was charged with conspiracy to sell narcotics. Without Massiah's (D) knowledge, Colson agreed to cooperate with federal agents in their investigation of Massiah (D) and have a radio transmitter installed in his car so that federal agents could overhear conversations taking place there. During one such conversation with Colson, Massiah (D) made incriminating statements. The district court admitted the statements at trial, which resulted in Massiah's (D) conviction. The court of appeals affirmed, and Massiah (D) appealed.

ISSUE: Does the Sixth Amendment forbid the use at trial of incriminating statements deliberately elicited from an accused by government agents after the accused has been indicted and in the absence of counsel?

HOLDING AND DECISION: (Stewart, J.) Yes. The Sixth Amendment forbids the use at trial of incriminating statements deliberately elicited from an accused by government agents after the accused has been indicted and in the absence of counsel. Under the Fourteenth Amendment, the right of an accused to counsel in a state criminal adversarial proceeding commences no later than upon indictment of the accused. A contrary ruling might deny an accused "effective representation by counsel at the only stage when legal aid and advice would help him." The Sixth Amendment's specific guarantee of the right to assistance of counsel applies directly to this federal proceeding. The interrogation need not take place in a police station. For the rule to have any efficacy, it must also apply to the indirect and surreptitious interrogation conducted here. This is especially true, since Massiah (D) was more seriously imposed upon in that he did not even know he was being interrogated. The continued investigation of Massiah (D) following his indictment was within Sixth Amendment strictures. The introduction at trial of the incriminating statements deliberately elicited from Massiah (D) by authorities in the absence of his counsel was not. Reversed.

DISSENT: (White, J.) Since the new rule would exclude all admissions made to the police, no matter how voluntary and reliable, the requirement of counsel's presence or approval would seem to rest upon the probability that counsel would foreclose any admissions at all. This is nothing more than a thinly disguised constitutional policy of minimizing or entirely prohibiting the use in evidence of voluntary out-of-court admissions and confessions made by the accused. The Court's newly fashioned exclusionary principle goes far beyond the constitutional privilege against self-incrimination, which neither requires nor suggests the barring of voluntary pretrial admissions. A wiser rule that should be used, instead of the one announced by the majority, is to consider the absence of counsel as one of several factors by which voluntariness is to be judged.

EDITOR'S ANALYSIS: In Massiah, the Supreme Court, for the first time, held that the right to counsel arises prior to trial in a criminal proceeding. The Sixth Amendment right to counsel at trial discussed in Massiah must be clearly distinguished from the prophylactic right to counsel during interrogation articulated in Miranda. In fact, Massiah, decided in 1964, preceded Miranda by two years.

[For more information on Sixth Amendment interrogation rights, see Casenote Law Outline on Criminal Procedure, Chapter 20, § I, The Massiah Right-to-Counsel Doctrine.]

NOTES:

MIRANDA v. ARIZONA
384 U.S. 436 (1966).

NATURE OF CASE: Appeal from a conviction of kidnapping and rape.

FACT SUMMARY: Miranda (D) contended that his written and oral confessions should not be admitted into evidence because he was not advised of his right to consult with an attorney and to have one present during the interrogation.

CONCISE RULE OF LAW: A defendant's statement may not be offered into evidence if it results from custodial interrogation of the defendant by the government unless warnings under the Fifth Amendment have been given to the defendant.

FACTS: The police arrested Miranda (D) for kidnapping and rape and took him to the police station, where he was identified by a complaining witness. The officers then took Miranda (D) to an interrogation room to answer some questions. The officers did not advise Miranda (D) that he had the right to have an attorney present. Two hours later, the officers obtained a written confession from Miranda (D). At the top of the statement was a typed paragraph stating that the confession was made voluntarily, without threats or promises of immunity, and with full knowledge of his legal rights. At his trial, the written confession was admitted into evidence over Miranda's (D) objection, and the officers testified to the prior oral confession made by Miranda (D) during the interrogation. Miranda (D) was found guilty, and he appealed, arguing that he should have been informed of his right to have an attorney present during interrogation.

ISSUE: Unless warnings under the Fifth Amendment have been given to the defendant, may a defendant's statement be offered into evidence if it results from custodial interrogation of the defendant by the government?

HOLDING AND DECISION: (Warren, C.J.) No. A defendant's statement may not be offered into evidence if it results from custodial interrogation of the defendant by the government unless warnings under the Fifth Amendment have been given to the defendant. The defendant must be informed, prior to custodial interrogation, that he has the right to remain silent, anything he says can be used against him at trial, he has the right to the assistance of a lawyer, and if he cannot afford a lawyer, the government will provide him with one. Custodial interrogation shall be defined as questioning initiated by law enforcement officers after a person has been taken into custody or otherwise deprived of his freedom of action in any significant way. The defendant may waive these rights, provided the waiver is made voluntarily, knowingly, and intelligently. If, however, he indicates in any manner and at any stage of the process that he wishes to consult with an attorney before speaking, there can be no questioning. Likewise, the defendant may stop the questioning at any time and ask for an attorney. In addition, if an interrogation takes place without the presence of an attorney and a statement is taken, a heavy burden rests on the government to demonstrate that the defendant knowingly and intelligently waived his rights. From the testimony of the officers and by the admission of Arizona (P), it is clear that Miranda (D) was not in any way apprised of his right to consult with an attorney and to have one present during his interrogation, nor was his right not to be compelled to incriminate himself effectively protected in any other manner. Without these warnings, the statements were inadmissible. The mere fact that he signed a statement which contained a typed-in clause stating that he had "full knowledge" of his "legal rights" does not approach the knowing and intelligent waiver required to relinquish constitutional rights. Reversed.

DISSENT: (White, J.) The majority's decision leaves open such questions as whether the accused was in custody, whether his statements were spontaneous or the product of the interrogation, whether the accused has effectively waived his rights, and whether nontestimonial evidence introduced at trial is the fruit of the statements made during a prohibited interrogation. All of these questions are certain to prove productive of uncertainty during investigation and litigation during prosecution. For all these reasons, if further restrictions on police interrogation are desirable at this time, a more flexible approach makes much more sense than the majority's constitutional straightjacket, which forecloses more discriminating treatment by legislative or rulemaking pronouncements.

EDITOR'S ANALYSIS: The majority stressed that all confessions are not inadmissible and remain a proper element in law enforcement. There is no requirement that police stop a person who enters a police station and states that he wishes to confess to a crime. Volunteered statements of any kind are not barred by the Fifth Amendment, and their admissibility is not affected by the majority's holding in Miranda.

[For more information on Miranda rights, see Casenote Law Outline on Criminal Procedure, Chapter 19, §§ I-IX.]

NOTES:

RHODE ISLAND v. INNIS
446 U.S. 291 (1980).

NATURE OF CASE: Appeal from a suppression of statements.

FACT SUMMARY: Innis (D) contended that the police officer's comments were made in order to elicit a response by Innis (D), thereby interrogating him, in violation of Miranda.

CONCISE RULE OF LAW: There is no interrogation where comments by one officer to another officer about the dangerousness of the crime elicit a response from the suspect.

FACTS: Innis (D) was arrested for the gunshot murder of a taxicab driver and the armed robbery of another taxicab driver. The robbery victim identified Innis (D) in a photograph at the police station and told the police that Innis (D) used a sawed-off shotgun to rob him. When the police picked up Innis (D), he was unarmed. Three different officers advised Innis (D) of his Miranda rights. Innis (D) stated that he understood his rights and wanted to speak with a lawyer. Three different officers were assigned to drive Innis (D) to the police station, and their captain told them not to question, intimidate, or coerce Innis (D) in any way. While en route, one of the officers stated to the others that there were a lot of handicapped children in the area and voiced his concern that they might find the gun and hurt themselves. Innis (D) interrupted the conversation and told the officers he would show them where the gun was. Innis (D) was driven back to the spot where he was arrested and again given the Miranda warning by the captain. Innis (D) then told the captain the location of the gun. The Rhode Island Supreme Court held that the police's statements constituted interrogation and suppressed Innis' (D) statements. Rhode Island (P) appealed.

ISSUE: Is there an interrogation where comments by one officer to another officer about the dangerousness of the crime elicit a response from the suspect?

HOLDING AND DECISION: (Stewart, J.) No. There is no interrogation where comments by one officer to another officer about the dangerousness of the crime elicit a response from the suspect. The term "interrogation" under Miranda refers not only to express questioning but also to any words or actions on the part of the police that the police should know are reasonably likely to elicit an incriminating response from the suspect. Given the fact that the entire conversation appears to have consisted of no more than a few offhand remarks, it cannot be said that the officers should have known that it was reasonably likely that Innis (D) would so respond. This is not a case where the police carried on a lengthy conversation in the presence of the suspect or where the officer's comments particularly "evocative." Reversed.

DISSENT: (Stevens, J.) In order to give full protection to a suspect's right to be free from any interrogation at all, the definition of "interrogation" must include any police statement or conduct that has the same purpose or effect as a direct question. Statements that appear to call for a response from the suspect, as well as those that are designed to do so, should be considered interrogation.

EDITOR'S ANALYSIS: According to Justice Stevens, if the officer directly asked Innis (D) in the form of a question where the shotgun was so handicapped children could be protected, there would then have been an interrogation. It would appear that in determining whether there was an interrogation, the totality of the circumstances must be examined. Factors to be considered include the nature of the statements, the surroundings where they are made, and the duration of the statements, among others.

[For more information on interrogation, see Casenote Law Outline on Criminal Procedure, Chapter 19, § VI, "Interrogation."]

NOTES:

PENNSYLVANIA v. MUNIZ
110 S.Ct. 2638 (1990).

NATURE OF CASE: Appeal from judgment suppressing evidence.

FACT SUMMARY: Muniz (D) was convicted of drunk driving after failing to answer police questions regarding his address and age.

CONCISE RULE OF LAW: In order to be testimonial, an accused's communication must, itself, explicitly or implicitly relate a factual assertion or disclose information.

FACTS: After Muniz (D) was directed by the police to remain parked until his inebriated condition improved, he drove off. The police pursued and pulled Muniz (D) over. After Muniz (D) failed three standard sobriety field tests, he was arrested. The police videotaped Muniz's (D) ensuing interrogation. Muniz stumbled over questions asking for his address and age. Muniz (D) also failed to answer the question: "Do you know the date of your sixth birthday?" Muniz (D) failed to submit to a breathalyzer test. He was then advised of his Miranda rights. The videotape was admitted into evidence at Muniz's (D) trial and he was convicted of driving under the influence of alcohol. Muniz (D) filed a motion for a new trial, contending that the videotape and field sobriety tests should have been suppressed as self-incriminating evidence completed prior to Muniz's (D) being given Miranda warnings. The trial court denied the motion, holding that a driver suspected of driving under the influence may be requested to perform physical acts or take a breath test without violating his privilege against self-incrimination. The Pennsylvania Supreme Court reversed, concluding that the videotape should have been suppressed in its entirety. The United States Supreme Court granted certiorari.

ISSUE: In order to be testimonial, must an accused's communication, itself, explicitly or implicitly relate a factual assertion or disclose information?

HOLDING AND DECISION: (Brennan, J.) Yes. In order to be testimonial, an accused's communication must, itself, explicitly or implicitly relate a factual assertion or disclose information. This case implicates both the testimonial and compulsion components of the privilege against self-incrimination in the context of pretrial questioning. Because Muniz (D) was not advised of his Miranda rights until after the proceedings and statements that were both testimonial in nature and elicited during custodial interrogation were videotaped, they should have been suppressed. Here, the sixth birthday question required a testimonial response. The inherently coercive environment created by the custodial interrogation precluded the option of remaining silent. Muniz (D) could have incriminated himself either by admitting he did not know the date of his sixth birthday or untruthfully reporting a date he did not believe to be accurate. The content of his truthful answer supported an inference that his mental faculties were impaired. The incriminating inference of Muniz's (D) impaired mental status stemmed not just from Muniz's (D) slurred speech but also from the testimonial aspect of that response. However, Muniz's (D) answers to questions regarding his name, address, height, weight, etc. are admissible because the questions fall within a routine booking exception which exempts from Miranda coverage questions to secure an accused's biographical data. Similarly, Miranda does not require suppression of statements Muniz (D) made when asked to submit to a breathalyzer tests. Such statements were not prompted by an interrogation, and therefore the absence of Miranda warnings does not require suppression. Vacated and remanded.

CONCURRENCE AND DISSENT: (Marshall, J.) The "sixth birthday question" required a testimonial response from Muniz (D). The question constituted custodial interrogation because Muniz (D) was required to answer correctly, which would indicate lucidity; answer incorrectly, which would imply that his mental facilities were impaired; or state that he did not know the answer, which would also indicate impairment. Because the police did not appraise Muniz (D) of his Miranda rights before asking the question, his response should have been suppressed. The booking questions, like the sixth birthday question, required Muniz (D) to elicit incriminating responses. Muniz' (D) initial incorrect response to the question about his age and his inability to give his address without looking at his license gave rise to the incriminating inference that his mental facilities were impaired. Accordingly, because the police did not inform Muniz (D) of his Miranda rights before asking the booking questions, his responses should have been suppressed. In addition, Muniz' (D) testimonial statements in connection with the three sobriety tests and the Breathalyzer test should have been judged to be products of custodial interrogation. The police should have known that the circumstances in which they confronted Muniz (D), combined with the detailed instructions and questions concerning the tests and the state's implied consent law, were reasonably likely to elicit an incriminating response and therefore constituted the "functional equivalent" of express questioning. Thus, Muniz' (D) statements to the police in connection with those tests should have been suppressed.

EDITOR'S ANALYSIS: In Connecticut v. Barrett, 479 U.S. 523 (1987), the defendant agreed to talk to the police after he was given Miranda warnings. However, he refused to sign a written statement until his attorney was present. Barrett testified at trial that he understood the Miranda warnings. The court held that the defendant's oral statements did not have to be suppressed. Even though a request for counsel should be broadly construed, Barrett's statements to the police were not ambiguous and should be understood as he intended them.

NOTES:

MINNESOTA v. MURPHY
465 U.S. 420 (1984).

NATURE OF CASE: Appeal from a suppression of confession in prosecution for false imprisonment.

FACT SUMMARY: Murphy (D) contended that statements he made to his probation officer should be suppressed because the officer should have warned him of his privilege against self-incrimination before she questioned him.

CONCISE RULE OF LAW: A statement made by a probationer to his probation officer without prior warnings of his privilege against self-incrimination is admissible in a subsequent criminal proceeding.

FACTS: Murphy (D) was on probation after pleading guilty to a reduced charge of false imprisonment in a sex case. The terms of Murphy's (D) probation required, among other things, that he participate in a treatment program for sexual offenders at Alpha House, report to his probation officer, and be truthful with the probation officer. An Alpha House counselor informed the probation officer that during the course of treatment, Murphy (D) had admitted to a rape and murder in 1974. The probation officer then asked Murphy (D) to meet with her. At the meeting, the officer told Murphy (D) of the information she received and expressed her belief that this information showed his continued need for treatment. Murphy (D) admitted that he had committed the rape and murder but told the officer that further treatment was unnecessary because several extenuating circumstances explained the prior crimes. The officer relayed this information to the authorities. Murphy (D) sought to suppress testimony concerning his confession. The trial court found that he was not "in custody" at the time of the statement, and that the confession was neither compelled nor involuntary. The Minnesota Supreme Court reversed.

ISSUE: Is a statement made by a probationer to his probation officer without prior warnings of his privilege against self-incrimination admissible in a subsequent criminal proceeding?

HOLDING AND DECISION: (White, J.) Yes. A statement made by a probationer to his probation officer without prior warnings of his privilege against self-incrimination is admissible in a subsequent criminal proceeding. Since Murphy (D) revealed incriminating information instead of timely asserting his Fifth Amendment privilege, his disclosures were not compelled incriminations. Custodial arrest is said to convey to the suspect a message that he has no choice but to submit to the officer's will and to confess. It is unlikely that a probation interview, arranged by appointment at a mutually convenient time, would give rise to a similar impression. In addition, there was no direct evidence that Murphy (D) confessed because he feared that his probation would be revoked if he remained silent, and, even if he did believe it, that belief would not have been reasonable. Because Murphy (D) had not been compelled to incriminate himself, he could not successfully invoke the privilege to prevent the information he volunteered to his probation officer from being used against him in a criminal prosecution. Reversed.

DISSENT: (Marshall, J.) The majority erred when it suggested that, to claim the benefit of the Fifth Amendment, a person who made self-incriminating statements after being threatened with a penalty if he remained silent must show that his apprehension that the state would carry out its promise was objectively "reasonable." It is clear that the threat alone is sufficient to render all subsequent testimony "compelled." The majority also erred when it implied that a defendant has a duty to prove that the state's threat, and not some other motivation, prompted his confession. The defendant need only prove that the state presented him with a constitutionally impermissible choice and that he thereupon incriminated himself.

EDITOR'S ANALYSIS: A state may require a probationer to appear and discuss matters that affect his probationary status; such a requirement, without more, does not give rise to a self-executing privilege. The result may be different if the questions put to the probationer, however relevant to his probationary status, call for answers that would incriminate him in a pending or later criminal prosecution. The questions directed at Murphy (D) were only about matters concerning his probationary status, and did not require him to choose between making incriminating statements and jeopardizing his conditional liberty or remaining silent and preserving his conditional liberty.

[For more information on interrogation, see Casenote Law Outline on Criminal Procedure, Chapter 19, § I, Miranda in Historical Context.]

NOTES:

ILLINOIS v. PERKINS
110 S. Ct. 2394 (1990).

NATURE OF CASE: Appeal from suppression of statements in prosecution for murder.

FACT SUMMARY: Perkins (D) contended that statements made to an undercover officer in jail should be suppressed because his Fifth Amendment privilege against self-incrimination was violated under the terms in Miranda.

CONCISE RULE OF LAW: Miranda warnings are not required when the suspect is unaware that he is speaking to a law enforcement officer and gives a voluntary statement.

FACTS: Parisi, an undercover agent, was placed in the cell of Perkins (D), who was incarcerated on charges unrelated to the subject of the agent's investigation. Parisi's investigation arose from information given to him about an unsolved murder by Charlton, a former cellmate of Perkins (D). Charlton claimed that Perkins (D) told him in detail about a murder he had committed while the two of them were incarcerated together. Parisi and Charlton posed as prisoners and were placed in the same cellblock where Perkins (D) was being held. Soon thereafter, Parisi and Charlton got Perkins (D) to describe at length the events of the murder in question. Parisi did not give Miranda warnings before the conversation. Perkins (D) was charged with murder. Perkins (D) moved to suppress the statements made to Parisi in the jail. The trial court granted the motion to suppress, and the state of Illinois (P) appealed. The Appellate Court of Illinois affirmed, holding that Miranda v. Arizona, 384 U.S. 436 (1966), prohibits all undercover contacts with incarcerated suspects which are reasonably likely to elicit an incriminating response. Illinois (P) appealed.

ISSUE: Are Miranda warnings required when the suspect is unaware that he is speaking to a law enforcement officer and gives a voluntary statement?

HOLDING AND DECISION: (Kennedy, J.) No. Miranda warnings are not required when the suspect is unaware that he is speaking to a law enforcement officer and gives a voluntary statement. Conversations between suspects and undercover agents do not implicate the concerns underlying Miranda. The essential ingredients of a "police-dominated atmosphere" and compulsion are not present when an incarcerated person speaks freely to someone whom he believes to be a fellow inmate. Coercion is determined from the perspective of the suspect. When a suspect considers himself in the company of cellmates and not officers, the coercive atmosphere is lacking. Ploys to mislead a suspect or lull him into a false sense of security that do not rise to the level of compulsion or coercion to speak are not within Miranda's concerns. Therefore, Perkins' (D) statements were voluntary, and there was no federal obstacle to their admissibility at trial. Reversed.

CONCURRENCE: (Brennan, J.) While the majority has not correctly characterized Miranda in its entirety, the majority is correct that when a suspect does not know that his questioner is a police agent, such questioning does not amount to "interrogation" in an "inherently coercive" environment so as to require application of Miranda. However, the Constitution does not condone the method by which the police extracted the confession in this case, and a claim could be raised that the confession was obtained in violation of the Due Process Clause.

DISSENT: (Marshall, J.) The majority reached the contrary conclusion of Miranda in this case by fashioning an exception to the Miranda rule that applies whenever "an undercover law enforcement officer posing as a fellow inmate . . . ask(s) questions that may elicit an incriminating response" from an incarcerated suspect. This exception is inconsistent with the rationale supporting Miranda and allows police officers intentionally to take advantage of suspects unaware of their constitutional rights.

EDITOR'S ANALYSIS: The majority distinguishes this case from Mathis v. United States, 391 U.S. 1 (1968), where an inmate in a state prison was interviewed by an Internal Revenue Service agent about possible tax violations. No Miranda warnings were given before questioning. The Court held that the suspect's incriminating statements were not admissible at his subsequent trial on tax fraud charges. The difference between the two cases lies in the fact that the suspect in Mathis was aware that the interviewing agent was a government official and, therefore, might feel coerced.

[For more information on police interrogation, see Casenote Law Outline on Criminal Procedure, Chapter 19, § VI, "Interrogation."]

NOTES:

MORAN v. BURBINE
475 U.S. 412 (1986).

NATURE OF CASE: Appeal from reversal of denial of motion to suppress a murder confession.

FACT SUMMARY: The court of appeals reversed the trial court's denial of Burbine's (D) motion to suppress his murder confession made after a valid waiver of his right to an attorney because the police failed to inform him of his attorney's preconfession communications.

CONCISE RULE OF LAW: A prearraignment confession preceded by an otherwise valid waiver is not tainted by unrelated police misconduct.

FACTS: After his arrest on a burglary charge, Burbine (D) validly waived his right to an attorney prior to confessing to an unrelated murder of a woman. This confession, however, was preceded, unbeknownst to Burbine (D), by his attorney's attempt to contact him, whereby the officer answering the phone stated to the attorney that Burbine (D) would not be questioned. Later, prior to Burbine's (D) murder trial in state court, he moved to suppress his confession. The state court denied the motion, which was affirmed on appeal by the Rhode Island Supreme Court. After unsuccessfully petitioning the U.S. district court for a writ of habeas corpus, Burbine (D) appealed to the First Circuit Court of Appeals, which reversed and granted his motion. Moran (P), on behalf of Rhode Island, appealed.

ISSUE: Is a prearraignment confession preceded by an otherwise valid waiver tainted by unrelated police misconduct?

HOLDING AND DECISION: (O'Connor, J.) No. A prearraignment confession preceded by an otherwise valid waiver is not tainted by unrelated police misconduct. This rule follows from examining the underlying purpose of the Miranda rules and striking a proper balance between the competing interests Miranda recognizes. In respect to the former, the purpose of these rules is to dissipate the compulsion inherent in interrogation and, in so doing, guard against abridgment of a defendant's Fifth Amendment rights. Clearly, a rule that focuses on conduct bearing no relevance at all to the degree of compulsion experienced by the defendant during interrogation would ignore both Miranda's mission and its only source of legitimacy. In respect to the latter, given Miranda's recognition of the need for police questioning as an effective law enforcement measure as weighed against the need to provide a defendant with some protections against such an inherently coercive process, a rule requiring additional protection for conduct unrelated to this process would both be unnecessary for the protection of the Fifth Amendment privilege and injurious to legitimate law enforcement. In the instant case, since the police misconduct centered around activity unrelated to Burbine's (D) otherwise valid murder confession and since it did not offend the Fourteenth Amendment's guarantee of fundamental fairness, Burbine's (D) motion to suppress his confession was wrongly granted by the court of appeals. Reversed and remanded.

DISSENT: (Stevens, J.) Settled principles about construing waivers of constitutional rights and about the need for strict presumptions in custodial interrogations, as well as a plain reading of the Miranda opinion itself, overwhelmingly support the conclusion that a suspect's waiver of his right to counsel is invalid if police refuse to inform him of his counsel's communications.

EDITOR'S ANALYSIS: In Michigan v. Mosley, 423 U.S. 96 (1975), Mosley, who had been arrested in connection with certain robberies, was briefly interrogated; he then invoked his right to remain silent, at which point the interrogation ceased. Sometime later, a different police officer interrogated Mosley about a homicide. The second officer advised Mosley of his rights, obtained a waiver, and secured incriminating information. The Court found that Mosley's rights had not been violated, holding that Miranda does not literally mean that a person who has invoked his "right to silence" can never again be subjected to custodial interrogation by any police officer at any time or place on any subject.

NOTES:

OREGON v. BRADSHAW
462 U.S. 1039 (1983).

NATURE OF CASE: Appeal from reversal of denial of motion to suppress confession in prosecution for vehicular homicide.

FACT SUMMARY: The appellate court reversed the district court's denial of Bradshaw's (D) motion to suppress his confession to personal involvement in the vehicular death of a minor, even though he reopened dialogue about the subject matter of the investigation subsequent to invoking his right to counsel.

CONCISE RULE OF LAW: An accused waives his previously invoked right to counsel when he reopens dialogue about the subject matter of the criminal investigation.

FACTS: After his arrest on another charge relating to the vehicular death of a minor, Bradshaw (D) invoked his Miranda right to counsel before further detailing authorities on what he knew about the death. Sometime later, Bradshaw (D), while on his way to prison on the above charge, inquired of a police officer, "Well, what is going to happen to me now?" The police officer responded by saying, in effect, that Bradshaw (D) was free to remain silent and that any further discourse was of his own volition. Bradshaw (D), in turn, said he understood. Subsequently, Bradshaw (D) agreed to a polygraph test. After taking this test and being told that his denial of personal involvement in the minor's death outside of the above charge was not credible, he confessed to driving the vehicle under the influence and causing the minor's death. At trial, Bradshaw (D) moved to suppress this confession, which was denied but reversed on appeal. Oregon (P) appealed.

ISSUE: Does an accused waive his previously invoked right to counsel when he reopens dialogue about the subject matter of the criminal investigation?

HOLDING AND DECISION: (Rehnquist, J.) Yes. An accused waives his previously invoked right to counsel when he reopens dialogue about the subject matter of the criminal investigation. This rule presumes that this waiver is made voluntarily and intelligently and follows from a proper application of the principle laid down in Edwards v. Arizona, 451 U.S. 477 (1981), where this Court ruled, in effect, that an accused's invocation of a right to counsel disallows further police interrogation of him unless he initiates further "communications, exchanges, or conversations with the police." A recent restatement of this principle requires that before a suspect in custody can be subjected to further interrogation after he requests an attorney, there must be a showing that he initiated the dialogue with the authorities. However, even if an accused, after expressing a desire for counsel, initiates conversation with the police, the burden still remains upon the prosecution to show that subsequent events indicated a waiver of the accused's Fifth Amendment right to have counsel present during the interrogation. That is, the prosecution must show that an accused, after invoking his right to counsel, evinced a willingness to converse about the subject matter of his arrest. In the instant case, since Bradshaw's (D) question evinced a willingness and a desire for a generalized discussion about the investigation, his subsequent confession did not violate his Fifth Amendment right to counsel. Accordingly, his confession did not violate his Fifth Amendment right to counsel. Reversed and remanded.

DISSENT: (Marshall, J.) On these facts, it is not apparent that Bradshaw's (D) question could be considered to have initiated a conversation about the subject matter of the criminal investigation.

EDITOR'S ANALYSIS: In Fare v. Michel C., 442 U.S. 707 (1979), a juvenile was interrogated about a murder. After being given his rights, he asked, "Can I have my probation officer here?" The police officer said that he was not going to call the probation officer and, "if you want to talk to us without an attorney present, you can. If you don't want to, you don't have to." The juvenile agreed to talk and made incriminating statements. The Court found the statements inadmissible, on the grounds that Miranda had not adequately been invoked and that attorneys play a unique role in the criminal justice system.

NOTES:

DAVIS v. UNITED STATES
__U.S.__, 114 S. Ct. 2350 (1994).

NATURE OF CASE: Review of murder conviction.

FACT SUMMARY: Davis (D), while in police custody, made ambiguous statements during interrogation regarding his desire for an attorney.

CONCISE RULE OF LAW: Ambiguous statements made during custodial interrogation regarding the desire for an attorney may not preclude further interrogation.

FACTS: Davis (D) was arrested by police on suspicion of homicide. He was subjected to custodial interrogation after waiving his Miranda rights. At one point he stated that "maybe I should talk to a lawyer." When the police asked if this meant he was asking for a lawyer, he replied in the negative. Later in the interrogation he requested a lawyer, at which time interrogation ceased. At trial, statements he made after mentioning he perhaps should talk to a lawyer were introduced, over his objection. He was convicted of second-degree murder. This was affirmed on appeal. The Supreme Court granted review.

ISSUE: Do ambiguous statements made during custodial interrogation regarding the desire for an attorney preclude further interrogation?

HOLDING AND DECISION: (O'Connor, J.) No. Ambiguous statements made during custodial interrogation regarding the desire for an attorney may not preclude further interrogation. This Court has held that once a suspect clearly asserts his right to counsel, interrogation must cease. So long as the police have made it clear that the suspect has the right to remain silent and has the right to counsel, the suspect must unambiguously request counsel. Police should not be burdened with divining what a suspect may or may not have meant in an equivocal statement. Miranda and its progeny were never meant to be irrational obstacles to legitimate police investigative activity, and the rule urged by Davis (D) would be such an impediment. Here, the comment "maybe I should talk to a lawyer" cannot be considered an unambiguous request for counsel. Affirmed.

CONCURRENCE: (Souter, J.) In the present case, the fact that the police requested clarification from Davis (D) rendered their subsequent interrogation proper.

EDITOR'S ANALYSIS: The present case represents a refinement of Edwards v. Arizona, 451 U.S. 477 (1981). That case articulated a "rigid prophylactic rule" designed to determine whether the accused actually invoked his right to counsel. This is an objective inquiry. Invocation of the Miranda right, according to Edwards, requires, at a minimum, some statement that can reasonably be construed to be an expression of a desire for an attorney's assistance. As the Davis court interprets this rule, however, the Miranda right must be "clearly" expressed.

[For more information on custodial interrogation, see Casenote Law Outline on Criminal Procedure, Chapter 19, § VIII.]

NOTES:

BREWER v. WILLIAMS
430 U.S. 387 (1977).

NATURE OF CASE: Appeal of grant of writ of habeas corpus after murder conviction.

FACT SUMMARY: Following his arraignment, Williams (P) told police where to find his victim's body after police initiated a discussion on the importance of a Christian burial.

CONCISE RULE OF LAW: Once adversary proceedings have commenced against an individual, he has a right to legal representation when the government interrogates him.

FACTS: Williams (P), charged with murdering a little girl in Des Moines, turned himself in to the Davenport police. He was arraigned in Davenport and requested an attorney. The police sent to pick Williams (P) up were instructed not to talk to him about the case without an attorney present. On the drive, Detective Leaming, who knew Williams (P) was religious, initiated a discussion on the importance of a Christian burial for the victim. After the "Christian burial speech," Williams (P) took Detective Leaming to the girl's body. Williams (P) was convicted of murder despite his counsel's efforts to suppress all evidence relating to Williams' (P) statements during the auto ride. Williams (P) petitioned for a writ of habeas corpus on grounds that the statements and attendant evidence were obtained in violation of his Sixth Amendment right to counsel and should have been excluded at trial. The district court agreed. The appellate court affirmed, and Brewer (D), on behalf of Iowa, appealed.

ISSUE: Once adversary proceedings have commenced against an individual, does he have a right to legal representation when the government interrogates him?

HOLDING AND DECISION: (Stewart, J.) Yes. Once adversary proceedings have commenced against an individual, he has a right to legal representation when the government interrogates him. Williams (P) was entitled to counsel at the time he made the incriminating statements, and there can be no serious doubt that Detective Leaming set out to elicit information from Williams (P) just as surely as if he had formally interrogated him. Further, there was no evidence that Williams (P) waived his right to counsel. Williams' (P) consistent reliance upon the advice of counsel and his statements that he would only talk to police with an attorney present refuted any suggestion of waiver. Despite Williams' (P) express and implicit assertions of his right to counsel, Detective Leaming proceeded to elicit incriminating statements from Williams (P). This evidence violated Miranda and was inadmissible. Affirmed.

CONCURRENCE: (Marshall, J.) The heinous nature of the crime is no excuse for condoning knowing and intentional police transgression of the constitutional rights of a defendant. The Court rightly condemned intentional police misconduct.

DISSENT: (Burger, C.J.) This decision carries the exclusionary rule to an absurd extent, punishing the public for the mistakes and misdeeds of law enforcement officers instead of punishing the officer directly.

DISSENT: (White, J.) Williams (P) was fully aware of his right not to talk to the officers without the advice and presence of counsel. By voluntarily telling the officers where to find the body, Williams (P) waived this right.

DISSENT: (Blackmun, J.) The Court's holding that constitutional rights are violated whenever police engage in any conduct in the absence of counsel with the desire to obtain information from a suspect after arraignment is too broad.

EDITOR'S ANALYSIS: While both the Fifth Amendment and the Sixth Amendment seek to protect a criminal defendant from illegal interrogation, the significant difference between the Sixth Amendment right to counsel and the Fifth Amendment right against self-incrimination is that the Sixth Amendment right attaches after the initiation of formal proceedings. The right to counsel applies to any adversarial proceeding, as well as to noncustodial settings such as eliciting information from a suspect who is free on bail. This right may be waived only if the waiver is knowing, voluntary, and intelligent. The state has the burden of establishing waiver.

[For more information on adversary judicial proceedings, see Casenote Law Outline on Criminal Procedure, Chapter 20, § II, "Adversary Judicial Criminal Proceedings".]

NOTES:

MICHIGAN v. JACKSON
475 U.S. 625 (1986).

NATURE OF CASE: Appeal of grant of motion to exclude confession in murder prosecution.

FACT SUMMARY: Bladel (D) and Jackson (D), two defendants being separately arraigned on unrelated murder charges, sought to suppress voluntary confessions given after they had requested counsel but before counsel had been provided to them.

CONCISE RULE OF LAW: Police may not initiate any interrogation after a defendant asserts his right to counsel at an arraignment or similar proceeding without a valid waiver of the defendant's right to counsel.

FACTS: Bladel (D) and Jackson (D) were arrested on unrelated murder charges. At their arraignments, both men requested that counsel be appointed for them. Subsequently, after being read their Miranda rights but before counsel was provided for them, both men voluntarily confessed. At both Bladel's (D) and Jackson's (D) trials, the trial court overruled the objections of each to the admissibility of their postarraignment confessions, finding that their Sixth Amendment right to counsel had not been abridged. In both cases, the appellate court affirmed. However, in Bladel's (D) case the appellate court reconsidered and reversed. The Michigan Supreme Court held that the post-arraignment statements in both cases should have been suppressed, noting that the Sixth Amendment right to counsel attached at the time of the arraignments when both men requested counsel.

ISSUE: May police initiate any interrogation after a defendant asserts his right to counsel at an arraignment or similar proceeding without a valid waiver of the defendant's right to counsel?

HOLDING AND DECISION: (Stevens, J.) No. Police may not initiate any interrogation after a defendant asserts his right to counsel at an arraignment or similar proceeding without a valid waiver of the defendant's right to counsel. Edwards v. Arizona, 451 U.S. 477 (1981), stands for the proposition that an accused person in custody who has asked for the assistance of counsel is not subject to further interrogation by police unless the accused initiates further conversation. This rule applies with even greater force after a suspect has been arraigned. After the "suspect" has become the "accused," the constitutional right to the assistance of counsel is of paramount importance. The State's (P) suggestion that requests for counsel should be construed to apply only to representation in formal legal proceedings is without merit. Every reasonable presumption against the waiver of fundamental constitutional rights should be indulged. The burden of proof was on the State (P) to show a valid waiver was obtained. No such showing was made. Affirmed.

DISSENT: (Rehnquist, J.) The prophylactic rule of Edwards, designed to protect a defendant's right under the Fifth Amendment not to be compelled to incriminate himself, does not meaningfully apply to the Sixth Amendment.

EDITOR'S ANALYSIS: The Court has continued to blur the line between the Fifth Amendment privilege against self-incrimination and the Sixth Amendment right to counsel. In Patterson v. Illinois, 478 U.S. 285 (1988), the Court held that the giving of Miranda warnings was sufficient to warn the accused of his Sixth Amendment right to counsel. The Court went on to say that a waiver given after such warnings also constituted a knowing and voluntary waiver of the Sixth Amendment right to counsel. Under this decision, then, a waiver of a defendant's Fifth Amendment rights is effectively a waiver of his Sixth Amendment rights.

[For more information on waiver of the right to counsel, see Casenote Law Outline on Criminal Procedure, Chapter 20, § IV, Waiver of the Right to Counsel.]

NOTES:

McNEIL v. WISCONSIN
111 S. Ct. 2204 (1991).

NATURE OF CASE: Appeal from denial of a motion to suppress a confession.

FACT SUMMARY: In Wisconsin's (P) criminal action against McNeil (D), the Wisconsin Supreme Court, affirming the trial court, denied McNeil's (D) motion to suppress his police-initiated confession to a crime unrelated to the crime he had previously been arraigned for, where, during this arraignment, he invoked his Sixth Amendment right to counsel.

CONCISE RULE OF LAW: An accused's invocation of his Sixth Amendment right to counsel during a judicial proceeding does not constitute an invocation of his Miranda right to counsel.

FACTS: After McNeil (D) was arraigned for armed robbery at which time he invoked his Sixth Amendment right to counsel, he admitted, during a police-initiated interview while being confined, that he was involved in the commission of another, unrelated crime. Moreover, just prior to this admission, McNeil (D) waived his Miranda right to counsel. As a result, McNeil (D) was formally charged and later convicted on charges relating to this admitted crime, which was affirmed on appeal, despite his motion to suppress his statement. McNeil (D) appealed.

ISSUE: Does an accused's invocation of his Sixth Amendment right to counsel during a judicial proceeding constitute an invocation of his Miranda right to counsel?

HOLDING AND DECISION: (Scalia, J.) No. An accused's invocation of his Sixth Amendment right to counsel during a judicial proceeding does not constitute an invocation of his Miranda right to counsel. The Sixth Amendment right to counsel is offense specific; that is, it merely invalidates subsequent police-initiated, counsel-absent interviews with respect to the charge or charges under which it was invoked. As a result, the police are free to initiate interviews without counsel's presence that are unrelated to these charges. An accused's Miranda right, on the other hand, is not offense specific. Accordingly, once an accused invokes it, the police may not initiate an interview with him relating to any charge whatsoever unless counsel is present. Nevertheless, given the policies underlying the Sixth Amendment and the Miranda rule (governed by the Fifth Amendment), it would be unreasonable for this Court to imply a simultaneous invocation of the rights involved with both simply by an accused's invocation of his Sixth Amendment right to counsel, since their policies are far from congruent. Moreover, a simultaneous invocation of both rights in such a case would seriously impede justice, since it would work to deter uncoerced confessions from suspects, thereby thwarting the important societal interest in finding, convicting and punishing those who violate the law.

DISSENT: (Stevens, J.) Undergirding our entire line of cases requiring the police to follow fair procedures when they interrogate presumptively innocent citizens suspected of criminal wrongdoing is the long-standing recognition that an adversarial system of justice can function effectively only when adversaries communicate with one another through counsel and when laypersons are protected from overreaching by more experienced and skilled professionals.

EDITOR'S ANALYSIS: In Michigan v. Bladel, 365 N.W.2d 56, 67 (1984), the court notes that the average person does not "understand and appreciate the subtle distinctions between the Fifth and Sixth Amendment rights to counsel," that it "makes little sense to afford relief from further interrogation to a defendant who asks a police officer for an attorney, but permit further interrogation to a defendant who makes an identical request to a judge," and that the "simple fact that defendant has requested an attorney indicates that he does not believe that he is sufficiently capable of dealing with his adversaries single-handedly."

[For more information on the Sixth Amendment right to counsel, see Casenote Law Outline on Criminal Procedure, Chapter 20, § I, The Massiah Right-to-Counsel Doctrine.]

NOTES:

NEW YORK v. QUARLES
467 U.S. 649 (1984).

NATURE OF CASE: Appeal of grant of motion to exclude statements in prosecution for possession of weapons.

FACT SUMMARY: Quarles (D) sought to suppress answers as to the whereabouts of a gun given in response to police questions before he was given his Miranda warning.

CONCISE RULE OF LAW: Statements made by a suspect before Miranda warnings are given are admissible under a "public safety" exception if elicited by police because of a genuine need to protect the public.

FACTS: Police cornered armed rape suspect Quarles (D) in a market. When police frisked Quarles (D), they could not find the gun. Before reading Quarles (D) his Miranda rights, police asked him where he had hidden the gun. Quarles (D) told police. Police then read Quarles (D) his rights and asked him some other questions about the gun, which Quarles (D) answered. At Quarles' (D) trial for criminal possession of a weapon, the gun and Quarles' (D) statements regarding its whereabouts were excluded because the police had failed to give Miranda warnings. Quarles' (D) other statements were excluded as evidence tainted by the Miranda violation. The New York appellate court and court of appeals affirmed.

ISSUE: Are statements made by a suspect before Miranda warnings are given admissible under a "public safety" exception if elicited by police because of a genuine need to protect the public?

HOLDING AND DECISION: (Rehnquist, J.) Yes. Statements made by a suspect before Miranda warnings are given are admissible under a "public safety" exception if elicited by police because of a genuine need to protect the public. This case presents a situation where concern for public safety must be paramount. The Miranda doctrine need not be applied in all its rigor to a situation in which police officers ask questions reasonably prompted by a concern for public safety. The need for answers in such a situation outweighs the need for the prophylactic rule protecting the Fifth Amendment right against self-incrimination. Admittedly, creating a narrow exception to the Miranda rule lessens the clarity of that rule. However, this exception should not complicate the thought processes or the on-the-scene judgments of police officers for it will free them to follow their legitimate instincts when confronting situations presenting a danger to the public safety. Reversed and remanded.

CONCURRENCE AND DISSENT: (O'Connor, J.) The facts of this case provide no justification for creating an exception to the Miranda rule. However, because nothing in Miranda requires the exclusion of nontestimonial evidence derived from informal custodial interrogation, admission of the gun into evidence was proper.

DISSENT: (Marshall, J.) Miranda was not a decision about public safety; it was a decision about coerced confessions. Without establishing that interrogations concerning the public's safety are less likely to be coercive than other interrogations, the majority cannot endorse the "public safety" exception and remain faithful to the logic of Miranda.

EDITOR'S ANALYSIS: The decision in Quarles reflects a judicial trend away from the strict application of Miranda. Some experts propose a return to a modified voluntariness standard which would examine the totality of the circumstances in a given situation to determine whether a suspect's pre-Miranda warning statements were coerced. Ideally such an approach would embody the ideology of Miranda by balancing the need to interrogate suspects with the desire to minimize abusive state practices. However, the return to the voluntariness standard raises the same factual problems of determining whether a suspect's statements were coerced that caused the Court to create the bright line Miranda rule in the first place.

[For more information on exceptions to the Miranda rule, see Casenote Law Outline on Criminal Procedure, Chapter 19, § VII, Exceptions to the Miranda Rule.]

NOTES:

OREGON v. ELSTAD
470 U.S. 298 (1985).

NATURE OF CASE: Appeal of grant of motion to exclude confession in prosecution for burglary.

FACT SUMMARY: Elstad (D) sought to exclude a signed confession given after the administration of Miranda warnings, claiming the confession was tainted by a prior confession given before police administered the warnings.

CONCISE RULE OF LAW: A voluntary confession given after Miranda warnings are administered is not tainted by a first confession given prior to such warnings.

FACTS: Before administering Miranda warnings to burglary suspect Elstad (D), police asked him if he knew anything about the burglary. Elstad (D) replied "I was there." Later, after being warned of his Miranda rights, Elstad (D) signed a full confession. At trial, Elstad (D) moved to suppress both confessions, contending that his initial pre-Miranda warning oral confession tainted the subsequent confession as fruit of the poisonous tree. The trial court excluded the initial confession as a violation of Miranda but admitted the later confession. Elstad (D) was found guilty of burglary in the first degree. The appellate court reversed on grounds that there was not a sufficient break in the stream of events between the inadmissible statement and the written confession to insulate the latter statement from the effect of the former.

ISSUE: Is a voluntary confession given after Miranda warnings are administered tainted by a first confession given prior to such warnings?

HOLDING AND DECISION: (O'Connor, J.) No. A voluntary confession given after Miranda warnings are administered is not tainted by a first confession given prior to such warnings. It is an unwarranted extension of Miranda to hold that a simple failure to administer Miranda warnings, unaccompanied by any coercion, so taints the investigatory process that a subsequent voluntary and informed waiver is ineffective for some unspecified period. Although Miranda requires that the unwarned admission must be suppressed, the admissibility of any subsequent statement should turn solely on whether it is knowingly and voluntarily made. Elstad (D) argued that he was unable to give a fully informed waiver of his rights because he was unaware that his prior statement could not be used against him. However, this Court has never adopted the theory that a defendant's ignorance of the full consequences of his decisions impairs their voluntariness. Miranda warnings convey all relevant information, and thereafter the suspect's choice should be viewed as an act of free will. Reversed and remanded.

DISSENT: (Brennan, J.) This decision deals a crippling blow to Miranda. It is ridiculous to assert that the connection between multiple confessions is speculative and that a subsequent rendition of Miranda warnings enables the accused to exercise free will in deciding whether to waive or invoke his rights.

DISSENT: (Stevens, J.) This decision is inconsistent with the Court's prior cases and will breed confusion and uncertainty in future cases. Furthermore, it undermines the importance of a core constitutional right.

EDITOR'S ANALYSIS: This case continues the judicial trend of defining "voluntariness" in a way that does not favor the defendant. In the prior case of Frazier v. Cupp, 394 U.S. 731 (1969), the Court refused to find that a defendant who confessed after being falsely told that his codefendant had turned state's evidence did so involuntarily. The Court has also rejected the argument that a defendant's guilty plea was involuntary because the defendant was ignorant of the fact that his prior coerced confession could not be admitted into evidence. McMann v. Richardson, 397 U.S. 759 (1970).

[For more information on the Miranda Exclusionary Rule, see Casenote Law Outline on Criminal Procedure, Chapter 19, § IX, Miranda Exclusionary Rule.]

NOTES:

COLORADO v. CONNELLY
479 U.S. 157 (1987).

NATURE OF CASE: Appeal from order suppressing statements and confession in prosecution for murder.

FACT SUMMARY: Connelly (D), who suffered from chronic schizophrenia, contended that statements and a confession he made to the police should be suppressed because they were involuntary and violated his privilege against compulsory self-incrimination.

CONCISE RULE OF LAW: Absent governmental coercion, the Fifth Amendment privilege is not concerned with moral and psychological pressures to confess emanating from sources other than official coercion.

FACTS: Connelly (D) approached a Denver police officer and stated that he had murdered someone. The officer advised Connelly (D) that he had the right to remain silent. Connelly (D) stated that he understood his rights and still wanted to talk. He then confessed to the murder of a young girl whom he had killed in Denver in November 1982. Under Connelly's (D) sole direction, he led police to the scene and pointed out the exact location of the murder. Throughout the entire episode, the officers perceived no indication that Connelly (D) was suffering from any kind of mental illness. The next day, during an interview with the public defender's office, Connelly (D) became visibly disoriented, stating for the first time that "voices" had told him to come to Denver and confess. At a preliminary hearing, Connelly (D) moved to suppress all of his statements. A psychiatrist testified that Connelly (D) was suffering from chronic schizophrenia and in a psychotic state at least as of the day before he confessed. On the basis of this evidence, the trial court suppressed Connelly's (D) statements because they were involuntary and his mental state vitiated his attempted waiver of the right to counsel and the privilege against compulsory self-incrimination. The Colorado Supreme Court affirmed. The State (P) appealed.

ISSUE: Absent governmental coercion, is the Fifth Amendment privilege concerned about moral and psychological pressures to confess emanating from sources other than official coercion?

HOLDING AND DECISION: (Rehnquist, C.J.) No. Absent governmental coercion, the Fifth Amendment privilege is not concerned with moral and psychological pressures to confess emanating from sources other than official coercion. Absent police conduct causally related to the confession, there is simply no basis for concluding that any state actor has deprived a criminal defendant of due process of law. Only if the Supreme Court were to establish a new constitutional right — the right of a criminal defendant to confess to his crime only when totally rational and properly motivated — could Connelly's (D) present claim be sustained. Therefore, coercive police activity is a necessary predicate to the finding that a confession is not "voluntary" within the meaning of the Due Process Clause of the Fourteenth Amendment, and, thus, the taking of Connelly's (D) statements and their admission into evidence did not violate his rights. Reversed.

DISSENT: (Brennan, J.) The Court denied Connelly (D) his fundamental right to make a vital choice with a sane mind, a determination that could allow the State (P) to deprive him of liberty or even life. The use of a mentally ill person's involuntary confession is antithetical to the notion of fundamental fairness embodied in the Due Process Clause. The absence of police wrongdoing should not, by itself, determine the voluntariness of a confession by a mentally ill person. Until this case, this Court has never upheld the admission of a confession that did not reflect the exercise of free will.

EDITOR'S ANALYSIS: On the issue of Miranda, the Court also reversed the Colorado Supreme Court's decision that the state must bear its burden of proving waiver of Miranda rights by "clear and convincing evidence." Chief Justice Rehnquist pointed to the Supreme Court's holding in Lego v. Twomey, 404 U.S. 477 (1972), and reaffirmed that holding in the case at hand: whenever the state bears the burden of proof in a motion to suppress a statement that the defendant claims was obtained in violation of the Miranda doctrine, it need prove waiver only by a preponderance of the evidence.

NOTES:

NOTES

CHAPTER 10
ADMINISTRATION OF THE EXCLUSIONARY RULES

QUICK REFERENCE RULES OF LAW

1. **Impeachment with Unconstitutionally Obtained Evidence.** An assertion by a defendant on direct-examination that he had never possessed any narcotics opens the door on cross-examination solely for the purpose of impeaching the defendant's credibility as to evidence of narcotics unlawfully seized in an earlier proceeding. (Walder v. United States)

2. **Impeachment with Unconstitutionally Obtained Evidence.** The government may use evidence which is inadmissible in a case to impeach a defendant's testimony bearing directly on the crimes charged. (Harris v. New York)

3. **Impeachment with Unconstitutionally Obtained Evidence.** Evidence suppressed by an illegal search and seizure may be used to impeach a defendant's false trial testimony, given in response to proper cross-examination, where the evidence does not squarely contradict the defendant's testimony on direct examination. (United States v. Havens)

4. **Harmless Constitutional Error.** A codefendant's confession implicating a defendant in violation of Bruton is deemed harmless error under the Chapman rule when the other evidence of the defendant's guilt is so overwhelming that there is no reasonable doubt that the jury would have convicted the defendant even without the inadmissible confession. (Harrington v. California)

5. **Coerced Confessions.** Admission of a coerced confession may be harmless if it appears beyond a reasonable doubt that its admission did not contribute to the verdict obtained. (Arizona v. Fulminate)

    [For more information on coerced confessions, see Casenote Law Outline on Criminal Procedure, Chapter 18, § I, General Principles.]

6. **Inevitable Discovery.** If the prosecution can establish by a preponderance of the evidence that the information sought ultimately or inevitably would have been discovered by lawful means, the information is admissible despite its having been discovered by unlawful means, although not in bad faith. (Nix v. Williams)

NOTES

WALDER v. UNITED STATES
347 U.S. 62 (1954).

NATURE OF CASE: Appeal from conviction of narcotic transactions.

FACT SUMMARY: Walder (D) contended that cross-examination by the Government (P) about narcotics that were unlawfully seized from his home in a prior case was unconstitutional.

CONCISE RULE OF LAW: An assertion by a defendant on direct-examination that he had never possessed any narcotics opens the door on cross-examination solely for the purpose of impeaching the defendant's credibility as to evidence of narcotics unlawfully seized in an earlier proceeding.

FACTS: In 1950, Walder (D) was arrested for possession of heroin. However, because of an unlawful search and seizure, the heroin evidence was suppressed and the case dismissed. In January 1952, Walder (D) was again indicted on drug charges. The only witness for the defense was Walder (D) himself. On direct-examination, Walder (D) answered that he had never sold, possessed, or used drugs before. On cross-examination, the Government (P) questioned him about the unlawfully seized heroin, and Walder (D) denied that any narcotics were taken from him at that time. The Government (P) then put on the stand the officers who participated in the unlawful search and seizure and the chemist who tested the heroin. The trial judge admitted the evidence but carefully charged the jury that it was not to be used to determine whether Walder (D) had committed the current offenses but solely for the purpose of impeaching his credibility. Walder (D) was convicted, and the Court of Appeals for the Eighth Circuit affirmed.

ISSUE: Does an assertion by a defendant on direct-examination that he had never possessed any narcotics open the door on cross-examination solely for the purpose of impeaching the defendant's credibility as to evidence of narcotics unlawfully seized in an earlier proceeding?

HOLDING AND DECISION: (Frankfurter, J.) Yes. An assertion by a defendant on direct-examination that he had never possessed any narcotics opens the door on cross-examination solely for the purpose of impeaching the defendant's credibility as to evidence of narcotics unlawfully seized in an earlier proceeding. It is one thing to say that the government cannot make an affirmative use of evidence unlawfully obtained. It is quite another to say that the defendant can turn the illegal method by which evidence in government possession was obtained to his own advantage and provide himself with a shield against contradictions of his untruths. Such an extension of the exclusionary rule would be a perversion of the Fourth Amendment. Affirmed.

EDITOR'S ANALYSIS: If Walder's (D) attorney omitted the prior drug use or possession question, the Government (P) would never have had the opportunity to bring up the prior case. This case is consistent with the Federal Rules of Evidence (character evidence and impeachment). Opposing counsel cannot question a defendant about specific instances of conduct that go toward his character unless the defendant "opens the door" by stating that his character is intact and that he never engaged in certain activities.

NOTES:

HARRIS v. NEW YORK
401 U.S. 222 (1971).

NATURE OF CASE: Petition for writ after conviction for selling narcotics.

FACT SUMMARY: The government used prior statements of Harris (D) which had been obtained in violation of Miranda to impeach his testimony. The statements concerned the transaction for which Harris (D) was prosecuted.

CONCISE RULE OF LAW: The government may use evidence which is inadmissible in a case to impeach a defendant's testimony bearing directly on the crimes charged.

FACTS: The government's chief witness at Harris' (D) trial was an undercover police officer who testified as to two narcotic transactions with Harris (D). Harris (D) took the stand and denied having made the sales. The government, on cross-examination, asked Harris (D) whether he remembered making certain prior statements. Harris (D) responded that he did not remember any of the statements recited by the prosecutor. The statements contradicted Harris' (D) direct testimony. They had been obtained in violation of Miranda and so were inadmissible as evidence of Harris' (D) guilt. The trial judge so instructed the jury and informed them that the statements could be considered only in passing on Harris' (D) credibility.

ISSUE: Can a defendant's statement to the police, which was obtained in violation of Miranda and is inadmissible to establish the prosecution's case in chief against defendant, be used to impeach the defendant's credibility?

HOLDING AND DECISION: (Burger, C. J.) Yes. Some comments in Miranda could be read as barring the use of uncounseled statements for any purpose, but discussion of that issue was not necessary to the court's holding and cannot be regarded as controlling. Nor does it follow from Miranda that evidence inadmissible against an accused in the prosecution's case in chief is barred for all purposes. Such evidence was permitted for impeachment purposes in Walder. It is true that Walder was impeached as to collateral matters, whereas Harris (D) here was impeached as to matters bearing more directly on the crimes charged. But no different result is required. Having voluntarily taken the stand, Harris (D) was under obligation to speak truthfully. The prosecution did no more than utilize traditional truth-testing devices. "The impeachment process here undoubtedly provided a valuable aid to the jury in assessing Harris' (D) credibility, and the benefits of this process should not be lost, because of the speculative possibility that impermissible police conduct will be encouraged thereby."

EDITOR'S ANALYSIS: Harris (which was decided by a divided Court) lends support to lower courts which have taken a broad view of Walder. Walder, however, was based on a Fourth Amendment violation. Harris was based on a Fifth Amendment violation. The Harris majority viewed Miranda as serving primarily a deterrent function similar to the Mapp decision. Hence, it concluded that the deterrent function was adequately met by excluding the evidence from the prosecution's case. The dissent stressed Miranda's Fifth Amendment foundation and concluded that any use of unwarned statements would violate a defendant's Fifth Amendment rights. The Fifth Amendment, on its face, unlike the Fourth Amendment, prohibits the government from using "compelled statements" against a defendant for any purpose. Hence, it could be argued, Walder cannot govern the situation in Harris. It is also argued that impeachment by means of evidence obtained in violation of the Fourth Amendment is more defensible than use of evidence obtained in violation of the Fifth because the Fourth's exclusionary rule is a court-created device designed to deter the police, and as the link between police illegality and subsequent evidence becomes more attenuated, it becomes less likely that exclusion would affect future police conduct.

NOTES:

UNITED STATES v. HAVENS
446 U.S. 620 (1980).

NATURE OF CASE: Appeal from reversal of conviction for cocaine possession.

FACT SUMMARY: When Havens (D) denied on direct examination ever having been involved in smuggling drugs, the Government (P), on cross-examination, asked him if he had knowledge of having in his luggage a certain T-shirt, which it then introduced for impeachment purposes despite its having been the fruit of an illegal search and seizure.

CONCISE RULE OF LAW: Evidence suppressed by an illegal search and seizure may be used to impeach a defendant's false trial testimony, given in response to proper cross-examination, where the evidence does not squarely contradict the defendant's testimony on direct examination.

FACTS: Havens (D) was charged with importing and possessing cocaine after a Miami customs officer searched McLeroth, Havens' (D) companion, and found cocaine sewed into makeshift pockets in a T-shirt he was wearing under his clothing. McLeroth implicated Havens (D), who had already cleared customs, in the illegal activity. After Havens (D) was arrested, his luggage was seized and illegally searched without a warrant. The only thing found was a T-shirt with pieces cut out. Those pieces matched the pieces that had been sewn on to McLeroth's T-shirt, which were used to hide the cocaine. On direct examination, Havens (D) denied McLeroth's allegations that Havens (D) supplied him with the altered T-shirt and denied ever having been involved in drug smuggling. On cross-examination, Havens (D) denied knowledge of the T-shirt. The Government (P) then introduced the T-shirt to rebut his credibility. Havens (D) was convicted, but the court of appeals reversed, holding that illegally obtained evidence could be used only to impeach a statement made on direct examination.

ISSUE: May evidence suppressed by an illegal search and seizure be used to impeach a defendant's false trial testimony, given in response to proper cross-examination, where the evidence does not squarely contradict the defendant's testimony on direct examination?

HOLDING AND DECISION: (White, J.) Yes. Evidence suppressed by an illegal search and seizure may be used to impeach a defendant's false trial testimony, given in response to proper cross-examination, where the evidence does not squarely contradict the defendant's testimony on direct examination. The cross-examination about the T-shirt and luggage was closely connected with matters explored during direct examination. The Government (P) called attention to Havens' (D) answers on direct and then asked whether he had anything to do with sewing the cotton patches on McLeroth's T-shirt. Thus, the Government (P) did not "smuggle in" the impeaching opportunity in the course of cross-examination, and the ensuing impeachment did not violate Haven's (D) constitutional rights. Reversed.

DISSENT: (Brennan, J.) This case is not one of first impression. The identical issue was confronted in Agnello v. United States, 269 U.S. 20 (1925), which determined contrary to the instant decision that it was constitutionally impermissible to admit evidence obtained in violation of the Fourth Amendment to rebut a defendant's response to a matter first raised during the government's cross-examination. To avoid this consequence of the majority's new approach, a defendant will be compelled to forgo testifying on his own behalf.

EDITOR'S ANALYSIS: Justice Brennan feared that the majority's approach to the exclusionary rule would obscure the difference between judicial decision-making and legislative or administrative policy-making. In addition, he also feared the denigration of the Fourth Amendment's and Fifth Amendment's unique status as constitutional protections by treating the privileges as mere incentive schemes. The majority, on the other hand, placed the consequences to society as a whole from not allowing impeachment under the circumstances on a higher level than discouraging the use of illegally seized evidence when that evidence relates only to peripheral matters, the thought being that police will not be encouraged by this exception to engage in unlawful search and seizures.

NOTES:

HARRINGTON v. CALIFORNIA
395 U.S. 250 (1969).

NATURE OF CASE: Appeal from a conviction of attempted robbery and first-degree murder.

FACT SUMMARY: A codefendant's confession implicating Harrington (P) was erroneously admitted into evidence but was judged to be harmless error.

CONCISE RULE OF LAW: A codefendant's confession implicating a defendant in violation of Bruton is deemed harmless error under the Chapman rule when the other evidence of the defendant's guilt is so overwhelming that there is no reasonable doubt that the jury would have convicted the defendant even without the inadmissible confession.

FACTS: In an attempted robbery and first-degree murder case, four men, including Harrington (P), were tried together over an objection by Harrington (P) that his trial should be severed. Each of his three codefendants confessed, and their confessions were introduced at trial. However, only one codefendant took the stand and was subjected to cross-examination. Both Cooper and Bosby did not take the stand, but their confessions implicated Harrington (P) to some extent and were not subjected to cross-examination. Although Harrington (P) was not specifically named in the confessions, there were references to the "white guy" and references to Harrington's (P) age, height, and weight. Harrington (P) was the only white defendant; the others were black. Harrington (P) was convicted and on appeal claimed that the lack of opportunity to cross-examine Cooper and Bosby was a violation of his constitutional rights under Bruton and the Chapman rule. The California Court of Appeals affirmed.

ISSUE: Should a codefendant's confession implicating a defendant in violation of Bruton be deemed harmless error under the Chapman rule when the other evidence of the defendant's guilt is so overwhelming that there is no reasonable doubt that the jury would have convicted the defendant even without the inadmissible confession?

HOLDING AND DECISION: (Douglas, J.) Yes. A codefendant's confession implicating a defendant in violation of Bruton is deemed harmless error under the Chapman rule when the other evidence of the defendant's guilt is so overwhelming that there is no reasonable doubt that the jury would have convicted the defendant even without the inadmissible confession. In Bruton v. United States, a confession of a codefendant who did not take the stand was used against Bruton in a federal prosecution. This Court held that Bruton was denied his rights under the Confrontation Clause of the Sixth Amendment. Although Cooper and Bosby's confessions placed Harrington (P) at the scene and were used against Harrington (P), without cross-examination by Harrington's (P) attorney, others, including Harrington himself, put him at the scene. But apart from the codefendants, the case against Harrington (P) was so overwhelming that the violation of Bruton was harmless beyond a reasonable doubt. This Court admonished in Chapman against giving too much emphasis to "overwhelming evidence" of guilt, stating that constitutional errors affecting the substantial rights of the aggrieved party could not be considered to be harmless. By that test, this Court cannot impute reversible weight to the two confessions. Affirmed.

DISSENT: (Brennan, J.) In Chapman, it was emphasized that an error in admitting plainly relevant evidence which possibly influenced the jury adversely to a litigant cannot be conceived of as harmless. The majority, in this case, shifted the inquiry from whether the constitutional error contributed to the conviction to whether the untainted evidence provided "overwhelming" support for the conviction, thus putting aside the firm resolve of Chapman. Thus, the confessions of the other two codefendants implicating Harrington (P) in the crime might well have tipped the balance in the jurors' minds in favor of the conviction. Certainly, the state has not carried its burden of demonstrating beyond a reasonable doubt that these two confessions did not contribute to Harrington's (P) conviction.

EDITOR'S ANALYSIS: It should be noted that the Supreme Court has been unwilling to apply the harmless error doctrine to the admission of involuntary confessions, the denial of a defendant's right to counsel at trial, and the denial of a defendant's constitutional right to an impartial judge. The Supreme Court appears to be sending out the message that the aforementioned violations are so prejudicial to a defendant's right to a fair trial that they could never be considered harmless.

NOTES:

ARIZONA v. FULMINANTE
111 S. Ct. 1246 (1991).

NATURE OF CASE: Appeal from grant of motion to suppress confessions.

FACT SUMMARY: In Arizona's (P) criminal action against Fulminante (D) for first-degree murder, the Arizona Supreme Court, reversing the trial court's ruling, granted Fulminante's (D) motion to suppress two confessions he allegedly made in respect to the murder.

CONCISE RULE OF LAW: Admission of a coerced confession may be harmless if it appears beyond a reasonable doubt that its admission did not contribute to the verdict obtained.

FACTS: After his incarceration for federal charges relating to possession of a firearm, Fulminante (D) allegedly confessed to one Sarivola, an undercover FBI agent, that he sexually assaulted and murdered his daughter prior to his incarceration. Nearly one year after this alleged confession and after his release from prison on the firearms charge, Fulminante (D) allegedly made another confession to Sarivola's fiancee regarding the same incident. As a result of these confessions, Fulminante (D) was charged with the first-degree murder of his daughter, leading to his eventual conviction and a death sentence despite his pretrial motion to suppress the alleged confessions, which the trial court denied. On appeal, however, the Arizona Supreme Court granted Fulminante's (D) motion, holding that Fulminante's (D) alleged confessions were coerced and, thus, inadmissible, and ruling that the harmless error analysis was not applicable to coerced confessions. Arizona (P) appealed.

ISSUE: May admission of a coerced confession be harmless if it appears beyond a reasonable doubt that its admission did not contribute to the verdict obtained?

HOLDING AND DECISION: (White, J.) Yes. Admission of a coerced confession may be harmless if it appears beyond a reasonable doubt that its admission did not contribute to the verdict obtained. This rule merely applies the rule as laid down in Chapman v. California, 386 U.S. 18 (1967), which made clear that federal constitutional error may be held harmless if it is declared harmless beyond a reasonable doubt. In applying Chapman's rule to confessions, it is especially noteworthy that confessions are probably the most probative and damaging evidence that can be admitted against a defendant. Indeed, a full confession in which the defendant discloses the motive for and means of the crime may tempt the jury to rely upon that evidence alone in reaching its verdict. Accordingly, a reviewing court must exercise extreme caution before determining that the admission of a confession at trial was harmless. In the instant case, since the transcript discloses that a successful prosecution depended on the jury believing the two confessions, that both confessions were impeachable standing alone, and that the admission of the first confession led to the admission of other evidence prejudicial to Fulminante (D), Arizona (P) has failed to prove beyond a reasonable doubt that the admission of the coerced confessions was harmless. Fulminante's (D) motion to suppress the confessions was properly granted. Affirmed.

DISSENT: (Rehnquist, C.J.) The admission of Fulminante's (D) confessions was a classic example of harmless error.

CONCURRENCE: (Kennedy, J.) Although having reservations about the involuntariness of Fulminante's (D) confessions, the majority's holding that the confessions were coerced, inadmissible and, therefore, its admission did not constitute harmless error is acceptable.

EDITOR'S ANALYSIS: By opening the door to harmless error analysis, the above case creates the risk of erroneous harmless error determinations; and erroneous determinations are most likely to take place in cases in which there is strong independent evidence of a defendant's guilt. Thus, the above case may lead in practice, if not in rhetoric, to a harmless error standard for involuntary confessions that is similar to the lax standard rejected in Payne v. Arkansas, 356 U.S. 560 (1958).

[For more information on coerced confessions, see Casenote Law Outline on Criminal Procedure, Chapter 18, § I, General Principles.]

NOTES:

NIX v. WILLIAMS
467 U.S. 431 (1984).

NATURE OF CASE: Appeal of reversal of denial of habeas relief involving the inevitable discovery exception to the exclusionary rule.

FACT SUMMARY: Even without Williams' (D) leading the police to the dead girl's body, the girl's body would have inevitably been discovered, and, therefore, no constitutional violation occurred.

CONCISE RULE OF LAW: If the prosecution can establish by a preponderance of the evidence that the information sought ultimately or inevitably would have been discovered by lawful means, the information is admissible despite its having been discovered by unlawful means, although not in bad faith.

FACTS: In Williams' (D) murder trial, evidence was admitted as to the condition of a child's body when found by police after statements made by Williams (D) directed police to the scene. However, the tactics used by the police to obtain Williams' (D) statements were deemed unconstitutional. However, the trial court concluded that the Government (P) had proved that if a search by volunteers for the child's body had not been suspended and Williams (D) had not led the police to the child, her body would have been found within another three to five hours and in the same condition. Williams (D) sought and was denied in federal district court habeas corpus relief, the court adopting and applying the inevitable discovery exception to the exclusionary rule. The Eighth Circuit Court of Appeals reversed, stating that the lower court's record failed to indicate that the police did not act in bad faith. On appeal to the Supreme Court, adoption of the inevitable discovery rule was urged because exclusion of evidence seized unlawfully, although not in bad faith, would not deter police from making such seizures in the future.

ISSUE: If the prosecution can establish by a preponderance of the evidence that the information sought ultimately or inevitably would have been discovered by lawful means, should it be admitted despite its having been discovered by unlawful means, although not in bad faith?

HOLDING AND DECISION: (Burger, C.J.) Yes. If the prosecution can establish by a preponderance of the evidence that the information sought ultimately or inevitably would have been discovered by lawful means, the information is admissible despite its having been discovered by unlawful means, although not in bad faith. The inevitable discovery exception to the exclusionary rule was properly applied by the district court. It does not require a showing of good faith by the police. Exclusion of physical evidence that would inevitably have been discovered adds nothing to either the integrity or fairness of a criminal trial. From the record, it is clear that the search parties were approaching the actual location of the body, and had Williams (D) not earlier led the police to it, the body would have inevitably been found. The requirement that the prosecution must prove the absence of bad faith, as imposed by the court of appeals, would place courts in the position of withholding from juries relevant and undoubted truth that would have been available to police absent any unlawful police activity. Reversed.

EDITOR'S ANALYSIS: The Court rejected the court of appeals' application of a stricter clear-and-convincing evidence standard in the case above. Combined with the inevitable discovery exception, the judge in a case must be convinced only that it is slightly more likely than not that the evidence would have been discovered. Alternatively, "inevitable" may be interpreted as meaning a much higher degree of probability, and the preponderance standard may apply only to the historical facts upon which the inevitability conclusion is based.

NOTES: